Fantastic St.
Too much to do in one vacation!

By

John A. Boyd

Copyright 2016 John A. Boyd

Published By:

Create Space Independent Publishing Platform
Charleston SC

ISBN-13: (CreateSpace-Assigned)
ISBN-10:
BISAC: History / Caribbean & West Indies / General

Other books by John Boyd:

Caribs: The Original Caribbean Pirates & Founding Fathers of American Democracy (2013)

ISBN-13: 978-1482627138 (CreateSpace-Assigned)
ISBN-10: 1482627132
LCCN: 2013906486
BISAC: History / Americas / Native American

The Lost Pirate Treasure of St. Croix: Your Search for Billions Start Here (2013)

ISBN-13: 978-1490536392 (CreateSpace-Assigned)
ISBN-10: 1490536396
LCCN: 2013912438
BISAC: History / Americas / Caribbean & West Indies

Memoirs of Captain Sam Bellamy: The Prince of Pirates, St. Croix, 1716-1717 (2015)

ISBN-13: 978-1517768058 (CreateSpace-Assigned)
ISBN-10: 1517768055
BISAC: History / Americas / Caribbean & West Indies

Dedication

This book is dedicated to all of the hard working owners and employees of the businesses who collectively define our Tourism Product. Through their perseverance and hard work, they have managed to mitigate the effects of a deep recession following the collapse of our industrial base.

This dedication also extends to the volunteers that make our special events and world class sporting events a possibility. Without the help of volunteers, many of these events, which draw visitors to St. Croix would not be an economic possibility.

Acknowledgments

This is my fourth book and I am indebted to a small army of proof readers who have tried to improve my writing by teaching me rules of grammar and making sure I use the correct homophone. The most precious gift they could give me was time away from their busy schedules and I truly appreciate it.

My daughter, Dagny Evens, has consistently supported me on every project I have undertaken. She has two teenage daughter and is running a small business with her husband and still manages to proofread all of my books. My Friend Jerlyn Thomas has also been a consistent supporter. She has proofread several of my books and also, provided artwork for my book on the Caribs.

Over the years, there have been several others who have contributed there time including Melissa and Cameron Smith, John Nelson and Chuck Fischer. To everyone of them I also offer my wholehearted thanks.

Table of Contents

Chapter 1 1
  Introduction 1
Chapter 2 5
  When Should You Visit St. Croix? 5
Chapter 3 8
  Before You Come to Paradise 8
    Car Rental 8
    What About Using a Taxi 10
    Think About an Attitude Adjustment 11
    If your Cell Phone & WiFi are Important 14
Chapter 4 16
  Get books to read on the flight & on the beach. 16
    John A. Boyd 16
    Richard A. Schrader 18
Chapter 5 20
  Before Your Trip - Decide What You Want to Do!! 20
Chapter 6 22
  Things to Consider During Your Stay! 22
    Go to the Beach. 22
    Buster the Beer Drinking Pig 22
    Snorkel for Free 24
    Night Snorkel 28
    Buck Island is a must! 29
    Sunset Sail 31
    Buy Hand Crafted Jewelry 34
    Listen to the Music 37
    Interact with our Artists 38
    Take a Horseback Ride 40
    Scuba Diving 41
    Sports Fishing 43
    Charter a Plane 45
    Eat Local Foods 47
    Visit the Vegetable Market 48
    Visit our Cultural Celebrations 50
    Visit Local Restaurants 52
    Kayak Salt River 58
    Stand Up Paddle Board – SUP 61

    Hike St. Croix 62
    Adventures 74
    Visit the Wills Bay Baths 78
    Bird Watching 81
    Renew You Vows or Get Married 86
        Renew your Vows 86
        Getting Married 87

Chapter 7 89
    Attend Our Special Events 89
    Caribbean Night 89
        Caribbean Night at the Palms Resort 90
        Pirate's Buffet at Renaissance Carambola Beach Resort 93
    Jump Up 94
    West Walk 95
    The Caribbean Community Theater 95
    A Taste of St. Croix 95
    St. Croix Food & Wine Experience 96
    Annual Dine VI Culinary Week 96
    Crucian Christmas Festival 97
    St. Croix USVI AGRIFEST 100
    Mardi Croix 100
    The Guavaberry Festival 102
    Coconut Festival 103
    Starving Artists Day at Whim Museum 103
    Christmas Spoken Here 103
    The Annual Cruzan Latin Caribbean Pig Roast Festival 104
    The St. Croix Christmas Boat Parade 104
    The La Reine Chicken Shack Coquito Festival 104
    The SEAstock Annual Beach Party & Fundraiser 105
    Annual Johnny Cake Eating Contest 105
    Animal Jam 106
    Mango Melee at St. George Village Botanical Garden 106
    Oktoberfest 106
    Extreme Sports 107
        Dolphin's Sea Swim 107
        The St. Croix Scenic 50 107
        Annual Coconut SUP 108
        The St. Croix 70.3 Ironman Triathlon 108
        The St. Croix Coral Reef Swim 108
        St. Croix Marathon and Half Marathon 108

Chapter 8 110

- Do Something Silly 110
  - Build a Sandcastle 110
  - Live Life on the Edge 111
  - Go to The Crab Races 112
- YOLO!!! 113
  - Pick a Coconut 113
  - Climb a Rock Wall 116
  - Walk on the Wild Side 118

Chapter 9 120
- On the Serious Side 120
  - The Middle Passage Monument 120
  - Danish Colonial Buildings 128
    - Fort Christiansvaern 129
    - Fort Frederik 129
    - Estate Whim Museum 130

Chapter 10 132
- Smell the Flowers 132
  - Plants in the Garden 132
  - Books about St. Croix Flowers 134
  - Plants in the Wild 137

Chapter 11 147
- Your Personal Safety 147
  - Safely Walking and Hiking in St. Croix 147
  - Crime in Paradise 150

Chapter 12 155
- Villa Boyd on Judith's Hill 155
  - Upon Arrival at STX 156
  - Directions to Villa Boyd 156
  - Amenities of the Efficiency at Villa Boyd 157

Chapter 1

Introduction

I have lived in St. Croix for more than 35 years, about half my life, and I absolutely love it. Before that I lived in:

Connecticut, 1 year. I was too young to remember anything.

New Jersey, 26 years. Rural West New Jersey was beautiful in Spring, Summer and Fall and barren in Winter. It was hot in summer and had blizzards in winter. I remember buying my first air conditioner after 13 days over 100 degrees Fahrenheit. That heat wave lasted 16 days and 900 people died in New York City. In Winter blizzards, water pipes would freeze and break and you would be trapped in your house for days, sometimes without electricity or heat. The people were friendly.

Pennsylvania, 6 years. The Eastern rural area can be described the same as rural West New Jersey above. The people were friendly.

New York, 2 years. My wife and I lived on the shore of beautiful Lake Cayuga and this is the only place I lived that I absolutely hated. I arrived in Fall, and my first Winter there, the temperature did not rise above minus 20 degrees for over a week. The rest of the Winter was not much better. In the Summer, we were constantly attacked by biting horseflies and huge stinging mosquitoes. The people were as cold as winter and as biting as the bugs. I really don't know how I lasted a second year.

It should be obvious from the profiles above, I hate cold weather and cold people a lot more than I dislike warm humid weather. This provides an initial clue as to why I loved St. Croix immediately upon arrival. The people I met were friendly and caring.

The scenery of St. Croix can best be described as rolling hills very similar to the Northeast United States but covered with verdant green vegetation all year round. St. Croix weather is covered completely in the next Chapter but it is usually fantastic for all but six weeks a year. And those six weeks are better than winter for me because I swim every afternoon to cool off. It's not that it is really hot, it is just exceptionally humid with no breeze.

There are two types of visitors to St. Croix, Cruise Ship Passengers and

Hotel Guests. From what I can see, longer term visitors rate us much higher than Cruise Ship Passengers because they learn of many of the activities and events covered in this book and have a great time. When they arrive without a St. Croix bucket list, long term visitors still learn of all the wonderful places to go and things to do through the grapevine. However, sometimes this method is inefficient and they hear of something wonderful at the last moment and are sorry they missed it.

Despite living on St. Croix for thirty-five years, it took me over a year to research and write this book. I kept on remembering events and activities I had overlooked and some so new that I never knew they existed. Now that I have refreshed my memories of all the things I used to love doing, I am planning on one of the best seasons of my life as I try to live the next year of my life doing everything a tourist would do.

Cruise Ship passengers have a different problem. Unless they are lucky enough to meet someone on their cruise who has been to the island before and loved it, they will have a harder time learning from the grapevine. Their choices of cruise-related activities appears limited for St. Croix and on many other smaller Caribbean Islands. Cruise ship passengers will have to do a phenomenal amount of research on each island port they visit, which would give them prior knowledge of what they want to do when they arrive. Otherwise they can go on a cruise ship organized excursion, just randomly walk around the pier area and the beaches in the vicinity of the pier, or stay on the ship.

I checked with the Carnival website to see what they have to offer to passengers on St. Croix and frankly it is a little disappointing especially when you take time to read the reviews as I did. The highest ranking bargain I could find was the Frederiksted Half Day Sail and Beach Break with Jolly Mon and that excursion got a perfect 5 star rating from people over 65.

It seems younger people were upset by the extra time and effort spent with older people to assure their safe arrival and exit from the beach. I have to admit that some of the criticisms listed for other excursions are a little more valid so a passenger should read the Carnival ratings before choosing what to do.

Royal Caribbean International offers a list of Shore Excursions for St. Croix and their website shows many attractively described shore excursions but none are reviewed. All have the potential to be both interesting or boring depending on the companies and personnel they hire.

Holland America offers a number of excursions including many that overlap with the other two lines. Ratings seem to be more generous than Royal Caribbean when direct comparisons are made of shared excursions. Compliments and criticisms both seem reasonable.

I finally found a site called Cruise Critic, which rates the Island of St. Croix and many of the excursions and also allows everyone who wanted to see St. Croix on their own to rate their experiences. I read every single rating of three or below. And found three types of passengers who give St. Croix a poor to average rating.

The smallest group was one person who simply did not understand the rating system. He started his review by saying that this was the first time he ever gave a "1" rating but he had to do it because it was one of the most fantastic days of his life snorkeling at Buck Island.

A second group seemed to be miserable people who described nothing but positive experiences on the island including a wonderful time for the whole family and then condemned the whole island with a three rating. This is the equivalent of a teacher who gives nothing but praise to all children and then gives half the class a C average. There is nothing those students can do to improve their grades because they have no idea what they are doing wrong. This book is not meant to serve miserable people who will never have a happy day in their life and yet, refuse to acknowledge the reason.

This book is meant to help the group of island visitors who gave St. Croix an average rating because they have legitimate complaints or simply could not find anything to do. I cannot solve issues of poor customer service, but I can avoid mentioning the businesses that ruined your day in this book. I believe this book solves the problem of finding all the wonderful things you might want to do on St. Croix during your stay.

I wrote this book to dispel the concept that there is nothing to do on the island of St. Croix. It is not just cruise ship passengers who mimic this misunderstanding. We have many local people who work on this island who say there is nothing to do when asked by visitors. Some are not schooled in all that St. Croix has to offer and this book should help them to live more interesting lives and serve tourists with more accurate information. Some of these negative locals could also be miserable people who would say there is nothing they want to do in Miami, Philadelphia, New York City and Washington, DC. As previously stated, this book is not meant to serve miserable people who will never have a happy day in their life and yet, refuse to acknowledge the reason.

An Internet search of things to do can be exhausting. It was for me and I live here and have done almost everything I describe. I hope my book will be interesting and greatly reduce your search time whether you read it in it's entirety or just skim it.

I intend that future revisions of this book will be an interactive process. If you find a new exciting experience on St. Croix that I missed, let me know. If a business is closed or a new business opens, let me know. I will not respond to criticism on experiences not recommended in my book. If you do have a horrible experience, post your complaint on Trip Adviser and you will reach a much broader audience, including me.

I hope you have a wonderful time on your St. Croix Vacation and enjoy many of our varied activities. After your wonderful St. Croix Vacation, I hope that you have learned to love St. Croix as much as I do.

I can be contacted at villa.boyd@gmail.com

Chapter 2

When Should You Visit St. Croix?

Almost anytime you want is fine!

About five years ago, I put up a weather station at my house, Villa Boyd, and placed the data on the wunderground.com network. I posted it on line so everyone could get a real time feel for weather conditions on St. Croix.

From this experience, I found out that cheap weather stations, under $150, only last about a year and those that are under $300 do not last much longer. I replaced the equipment a few times but eventually lost interest. However, while my station was operational, I started paying more attention to our weather and had two epiphanies.

With my station off the air, the default weather link from Weather Underground says the weather today is pretty much the same as it was yesterday. Over any short period of time, like a season or three months, that is mostly true. The other observation is that we have four distinct seasons just like all the people from up north and you can learn to recognize them from the weather patterns and the seasonal flowers and fruit.

Generally, the wind direction for most of the year (nine months) is out of the East South East and is warm moist tropical air currents coming off the coast of Africa. Starting about November, the wind direction starts shifting to East North East and the cooler dryer air of the North Atlantic starts impacting our weather but not right away. First the winds have to cool the waters of our inlets and bays and the Caribbean Sea has to be slightly cooled before the full impact of the Christmas winds begins around the winter solstice on December 21.

From December until the end of May the temperature will average 78 to 82 every day with a daytime high around 84. From the winter equinox until the end of June is also the dry time of the year where you can expect a very insignificant shower about one day in four. Most of the time it will dry up for the day around 8 am in the morning.

During this period, our typical weather report says about 30 percent chance of rain. I finally found out that this means that 3 days out of ten, there will be at least 0.01 inches of rain or about 1/100 of an inch somewhere on the island from Point Udall to the rain forest. Most locals do nothing at all to protect themselves from the cooling effect of a very minor shower and many ignore the daily weather reports.

If it is half that amount, it is still counted as precipitation and the forecast is correct even though the amount is considered too small to record. So during an extended drought, the weather service would be correct by always predicting a 30% chance of rain for St. Croix because there is bound to be a light mist somewhere on the island. Unless you have the worst of luck with the weather on all of your vacations, I doubt that rain should be a concern of yours during the dry season.

In this period, the wind will be fairly constant at 13 miles per hour and about half that time, it will be above the average with a strong tropical breeze in the 13 to 18 mile per hour range. This is our growing season for American type vegetables as the weather matches spring and very early summer in the Middle Atlantic States. You absolutely have to love those six months of the year.

Summer in St. Croix is not the demon that most people think it might be. The wind starts coming from the East South East in February but that doesn't really change conditions until June. After that, the temperature rises to an average of 86 degrees, and it rarely goes over 90. During this period, the winds rise dramatically.

While the average wind speed rises to 14 to 15 miles per hour, two thirds of the time it is in the 13 to 18 mile range, which has a strong cooling effect. It is easy in the summer for a person to be very active and get dehydrated because it is so comfortable.

I have been telling my friends for years, that St. Croix is more comfortable in the summer than beaches from New Jersey to Florida. Best of all, summer is low season so hotel and rental rates are generally lower. No wonder St. Croix is turning into a wedding destination for adventurous young people. Very few businesses close during the summer months and most are less crowded.

For those of us who live here, the only bad news about weather includes rare hurricanes and six weeks of sweltering humidity. The worst of both of these occur sometime between Labor Day and Halloween. It's not really that hot during this period. In fact, the average temperature is actually dropping from a high of 86 to 82.

The issue is the wind speed is also dropping to a low for the year around 10 miles per hour, Also, forget about those cooling and comforting trade-winds in the 13 to 18 mile an hour range, they only occur about one third the time. The months of August through October are also the wettest part of the year and this is the most active part of the hurricane season.

Virgin Islands residents did not move to St. Croix to suffer in silence so there is very little effort to stoically suffer from the weather during that six-week period. During the other ten months of the year, we talk about family, friends, fun events and fun things we have done or are planning to do.

During those six weeks of fall that are relatively still and humid, people who don't leave the island, sweat and complain about the weather. We more or less jokingly blame each other for aggravating the weather gods and causing our hot and humid version of Hell. I try to ignore it, but no one really can unless you stay in an air-conditioned room for the duration of your visit.

Chapter 3

Before You Come to Paradise

Car Rental

While making your vacation plans, be sure to include renting a car as a priority. During peak periods, you can always find a hotel room or a private room through Airbnb, but it is not uncommon to find every rental car on the island is in use and that none are available for last minute arrivals. Trying to rely on our taxi system is generally a poor second choice. Specifics on taxis are in the next section.

At 84 square miles, St. Croix is the biggest of all the Virgin Islands. The island is 26 miles long and from east end to west end, there are places to explore and no one can visit them all in a week, let alone a one day cruise ship stop. If you have a car, you increase your flexibility. If it's raining west, head east. If it is raining from east to west, consider the rum factory tours. Having your own car increases your flexibility to do all that you want to do and insures you will have a great vacation or one day visit. If you reserve a car in advance, Budget Car Rental will deliver cars to cruise ship passengers near the pier. The rental companies on St. Croix are as follows:

Centerline

Location: Mid Island
Phone: 340 778-0450

Location: Christiansted Boardwalk
Phone: 340 713-0550

Location: Airport
Phone: 340-778-0441

Judi of Croix

Location: Delivered
Phone: 877-903-2123 (toll free)
Phone: 340-773-2123

Olympic

Location: Christiansted (Richmond Post Office)
Phone: 340 773-3000

Avis

Location: Seaplane
Phone: 340 713-1347

Budget

Location: Christiansted Sea Plane
Phone: 340 713-9289

Location: Airport
Phone: 340 778-9636

Gold Mine Car Rental

Location: Christiansted
Phone: 340-773-0299

Hertz

Location: Airport
Phone: 340 778-1402

Preferred Rentals

Location: Airport
Phone: 340 778-9744

Skyline Car Rentals

Location: La Reine, Mid Island
Phone: 340-719-5900
Phone: 877-719-5900

My family usually gets a reasonable deal from one of the first three on the list but when cars are tight, you may have to call everyone on the list. Most car rental agencies have simple rules and simple advice.

Rules:

Do not smoke in the car.

Clean the sand off yourself in the parking lot so you don't get excessive sand in the car.

If you plan to go off road or are staying along one of our many potholed roads or dirt driveways, rent a jeep.

Leave your bling and valuables at home or in your room. Stop at your room to unload your travel luggage before going out to eat. If your room is not ready, check your bag where you are staying.

My experience is that the rental companies are amazingly forgiving so just be polite and tell the truth if you have a problem or damage the vehicle.

MOST IMPORTANT: Drive on the left-hand side!

What About Using a Taxi

There is simply no way to avoid the pimple on the face of a St. Croix cruise ship stop. Those taxi drivers who wait at the Frederiksted dock on cruise ship days will occasionally work hard to ruin an island visit for cruise ship passengers with their ignorance of the island. They will charge the maximum and take visitors to places that they really don't need to see. Unfortunately, they are politically active and are well protected by the system so will still be here to abuse people even if they arrive on a cruise ship in 2045.

One reason that our best hotels get rave reviews is they cooperate with carefully selected taxi operators to serve their guests in order to ensure that no one is over-charged or left stranded and the driver is knowledgeable about all the wonderful things to do on St. Croix. These select drivers always support the hotels they are associated with, whether there is a cruise ship in port or not. They are the best dressed drivers with the best taxi vans.

Thank God, residents who love the island and tourists who visit St. Croix have developed their own ideas about places to visit and things to do that create a shared understanding of the meaning of a great St. Croix visit. If you follow the lead of those visitors who came before you, you will fall in love with St. Croix and not because it had seven flags.

On the positive side, bad taxi service may change. I met a young driver, Prince, of "Prince Taxi and Tour Service" who was describing the plants located in the rain forest to tourists he was guiding at the home of the Beer Drinking Pig. He was pointing out cocoa pods on the tree that are used to make chocolate.

He is also the only taxi driver I ever met who knew the exact location of St. Croix's last wooden bridge. It was built 350 years ago and has a Maltese Cross on each side leaving no doubt that it was built by the mysterious Knights of Malta. He told me he is working hard with other young drivers to improve the the knowledge and service of taxi drivers in the St. Croix Tourism industry. Phone 340-642-3811, email jaylingabriel@yahoo.com

There are a few other bright lights in the industry. I have known and worked with Frances M. Vazquez for over 25 years, I catch up with her at Hotels or when she is driving with youth groups on bilingual tours, Spanish and English. Phone 340-690-4045, email frances.vazquez@hotmail.com

It is unusual that I recommend a business that I have no knowledge of but there will be exceptions. Francis Jagrup gets rave reviews on Trip Adviser from both cruise ship passengers and tourists. Phone 340-332-5196, email fjagrup@hotmail.com

I see that other drivers are just starting to get good reviews on Trip Adviser for their knowledge of the island and fair prices but before I include them in this book I would like to see them have more than one positive review.

Meanwhile, if I were coming to St. Croix for only one day, I would try to hook up with one of the drivers mentioned in Trip Adviser who has served cruise ship passengers well. If I were coming for a longer stay and had a sense of adventure, I would rent a car or work with my hotel taxi driver who has been vetted by the Hotel.

Think About an Attitude Adjustment

As a visitor to the Caribbean, you may find a few things to criticize regardless of the island you choose to visit, but many of the things that go wrong are beyond the control of the business owners and even the staff. I love good customer relations, quality and a consistent offering of goods and services but sometimes these are beyond the control of everybody. At the extreme, even customer relations can be out of the control of the business after a very low standard for discussion has been set by an irate customer. I should know. I have run three business on St. Croix and have employed hundreds of workers over the past 35 years and understand the complexity of perfection.

In the restaurant business, there is often a conflict between quality and the continuity of supply and it is exacerbated by Caribbean conditions. When living stateside, I had owned a catering service and a couple of wine and cheese shops so was generally aware of the things that could go wrong with suppliers and employees. However, I was simply unprepared for the amplification in the number and duration of problems, which would be caused by being 1,500 miles from key suppliers.

In my first St. Croix Restaurant, I had no plans in place to solve a multitude of unexpected problem. I ran into problems with island wide shortages, poor deliveries, poor quality and more. Over the years, my restaurant's ability to serve the clientele was also disrupted by power outages, delivery truck breakdowns, hurricanes, tropical waves and flash floods.

The restaurant business in St. Croix is extremely variable. You could be empty one minute and slammed with customers the next. It is hard to tell people you are too busy to serve them food or cook a complex meal so you will probably never hear about the problems before you are seated. It takes time to cook a fresh fish or a perfect steak and no one wants to prep ahead and waste expensive food. If you only have a very limited amount of time, check before you are seated to ensure your needs for a quick meal can be met. There is usually a menu item that could be delivered in a hurry.

There is really not much that the owner or waitstaff can do to solve many problem other than to apologize about a lapse of quality or service that was unexpected and went unnoticed. On any given day, some menu items may be unavailable and other unavoidable problems can occur. If you are disappointed, don't scream at the staff but politely ask to speak to the owner or manger if you are not satisfied.

Even McDonald's has never completely solved the problem of delivering fast food in the Caribbean. Forty years ago, a friend in the Dominican

Republic told me the Caribbean adds a whole new dimension to the concept of fast food. The lines can be excessive at breakfast and lunch, but not every day so you never know before you arrive.

I would like to advise visitors that you will never correct a problem by screaming at an employee or insulting a business owner. Be polite and be patient. Often repeating a question because you do not understand our dialect in a belligerent manner will deteriorate into you being ignored. If you keep smiling, stay polite and confess a problem understanding Caribbean English, you just might get satisfaction.

Above all, avoid phrases like "that's not the way it is done back home." Before tourism developed around 1960, Caribbean people had survived for 400 years creating their own solutions with limited resources and unreliable outside supplies. Our ways are different, but as you will learn, they are not necessarily worse.

Some people are so sure that the way it is done "back home" is best for everyone that they sell their stateside possessions and move to paradise to start a business. Among business people in St. Croix, there is a standing joke that the easiest way to make a small fortune in the Caribbean Islands is to arrive with a large fortune and invest in a business. You are guaranteed to leave with a smaller fortune than what you had when you arrived unless you quickly adapt.

There is even a bumper sticker, which says; "We really don't care how you do it up North."

If you want to read a few funny books about life and business in the tropics, start with "Don't Stop the Carnival" by Herman Wouk. It is a comedy about escaping a middle-age crisis by moving to the Caribbean. Published in 1965, it was based on his efforts to run a hotel on Water Island in St. Thomas but many visitors still think it is true today. Also, read "A Salty Piece of Land," a 2004 novel by bestselling author and songwriter Jimmy Buffett. It is pure Caribbean fantasy about chemically challenged ex-pats living in the Caribbean Islands and all their adventures.

Another Tropical writer worth reading to help you get in the mood is Carl Hiaasen who tells stories that are filled with eccentric characters involved in adventure-filled plots. Most people living in the islands swear that they know a person who was the real person behind one of his zany characters.

Hiaasen's stories are mostly Florida based but still relative.

Finally, it is an old tradition in St. Croix that you greet all people you meet when walking on the street, especially if you make eye contact or if they greet you. It is also important in restaurants and at your hotel. Your hotel staff will love you right away and if something does go wrong, your new friends will try to solve the problem.

A simple Good Morning, Good Afternoon, Good Evening or Good Night will suffice. Even after 35 years, I have a hard time figuring the transition between afternoon, evening and night but it doesn't matter. I always get a big smile for whatever greeting I chose and the recipient responds with the proper salutation.

If your Cell Phone & WiFi are Important

Most Hotels, condominiums and guest rooms will offer WiFi, but check before you book your room. There are also various hot spots at coffee shops and a few bars but these are reserved for patrons.

Cell phone coverage is excellent for AT&T and fairly good for H2O and Sprint. There is usually no surcharge for using these carriers in St. Croix. Coverage is almost non existent for Verizon.

The work around is to buy a Go Phone on ebay and connect it to H2O on line or after you arrive. You can do it locally through a H2O stores on St. Croix. All H2O calls to the USA are free.

The local provider also has a web site where you can order online with them and see all they have to offer, but I don't know anyone who has taken this approach. www.mrsimcard.com/caribbean/s-stcroix.html

I checked on Ebay for a go phone and a cheap one can be found for under $30 and a used one for half that amount. It was a Samsung a157 AT&T Go Phone, 3G + $10 Refill Minutes Card, in a new Factory Sealed Package, which is suitable for unlimited talk, text & web nationwide. If you know what you are doing, you can probably connect to H2O online for a month by month service.

Be forewarned, occasionally there are disruptions in cell phone reception and WiFi coverage. They are usually for short periods of time but there is nothing much that your hotel or host can do to correct the problem once it has been reported. Just consider the loss of power or connectivity part of your great Caribbean adventure.

I have never been on any other Caribbean Island where I have not felt temporarily isolated from the outside world by loss of power or connectivity. It is at times like these that your smiles and good manners are most essential, especially if you would like any suggestions for alternate solutions. Not many West Indians on any of the islands will readily offer a suggestion to a mean-spirited person when they think they will be verbally abused if the suggestion fails.

Chapter 4

Get books to read on the flight & on the beach.

John A. Boyd

Of course I put this point in so I could plug my first three books, which cover two different subcultures that were part of island life but never researched deeply or discussed by local authors; the Caribs and the Pirates. My books, paperback or Kindle, are available from Amazon.com and at Undercover Books on St. Croix. They are also available at Caribbean Night at the Palms where I will be happy to autograph them or discuss them with you.

Caribs: The Original Caribbean Pirates & Founding Fathers of American Democracy (2013)

This is the story of Carib resistance to the European conquest of the Caribbean, which starts in 1493 at the battle of Salt River, St. Croix, United States Virgin Islands. By all historical accounts, the Caribs tried to avoid this battle and when attacked, lost to a superior force of well-armed conquistadors. For the next 55 years, the Caribs of St. Croix sought revenge and engaged in pirate raids and guerrilla warfare against the Spanish.

ISBN-13: 978-1482627138 (CreateSpace-Assigned)
ISBN-10: 1482627132
BISAC: History / Native American

The Lost Pirate Treasure of St. Croix: Your Search for Billions Start Here (2013)

My research tracks all the known pirate activity on St. Croix. Many pirates brought treasure to the island as did smugglers and merchants. It is well documented that Captain James Martel was killed on the island and half of his fortune lost to time so he certainly rates a Chapter.

Owen Lloyd took the treasure of Nuestra Señora de Guadelupe. Part of Lloyd's treasure was buried on the island and this stash became his bank until he was murdered in a Christiansted Bar. His story has been retold for centuries as part of Robert Luis Stevenson's book, Treasure Island. Only a small amount of this treasure remains on St. Croix so his chapter is small.

By far the biggest fortune that probably remains hidden on St. Croix is the vast amount of wealth amassed by Jean La Vasseur while Governor of Tortuga. During his reign, 1640 to 1652, he took a minimum of ten percent of all the prizes captured by the Buccaneers of Tortuga referred to as the Brethren of the Coast. He also collected taxes on all imports to the island. However, he cheated his partner in this criminal empire, Governor Phillippe de Lonvillers de Poincy of St. Croix, by keeping everything for himself. De Poincy retaliated by conquering Tortuga and claiming the fortune of La Vasseur as his own. After de Poincy's military conquest of Tortuga, this treasure is also lost to time. The research for this book brings that fortune to St. Croix where it is probably still well hidden.

ISBN-13: 978-1490536392 (CreateSpace-Assigned)
ISBN-10: 1490536396
BISAC: History / Caribbean & West Indies / General

Memoirs of Captain Sam Bellamy: The Prince of Pirates, St Croix, 1716-1717

The most successful pirate republic ever was on the island of St. Croix. From this location, three pirate captains worked together during the Golden Age of Piracy. The tale of Captain Paulsgrave Williams is a shared story with that of Captain Samuel Bellamy and is largely covered in this book. Their partner in crime, Olivier Levasseur, was perhaps the most successful pirates in the Golden Age of Piracy if the estimate of his wealth includes all of his Caribbean and African exploits. Despite their partnership, Levasseur and Williams never made the Forbes' list of the Richest Caribbean Pirates while Bellamy did. The reason of course is simple. Sam Bellamy's ship, the Whydah, was wrecked and the vast amount of his accumulated wealth was documented at the trials of the survivors. There is little documentation of the wealth accumulated by Levasseur and Williams.

Publisher: CreateSpace Independent Publishing Platform; (October 10, 2015)
ISBN-10: 1517768055
ISBN-13: 978-1517768058

Richard A. Schrader

I have known Richard Schrader, Sr. for more than 25 years and am not even sure how I met him. More than likely, it had something to do with the University of the Virgin Islands in St. Croix where I worked and occasionally taught.

I choose to write on the period before 1750 based on meticulous research because I love fact checking and digging up obscure sources. Richard has a focus on presenting and preserving the living cultural history of his youth before industrialization and mass media altered the fabric of life.

From my perspective, Richard Schrader is perfectly suited for his chosen focus on preserving the cultural heritage of St. Croix. He was born in St. Croix in 1935, left to join the U. S. Army in 1951 and returned to St. Croix in 1964. In 1965, he started working for the Bureau of Corrections at the adult prison in Richmond.

He returned home to St. Croix just before a massive industrialization program changed the fabric of society. In the next decade, the population grew from 15,000 to 75,000, a five-fold increase. The new people came from almost every Caribbean Island and many European and Asian Nations.

As the culture evolved in the years, which followed, it became more Pan-Caribbean than the culture of his youth as 80% of the population no longer had roots from St. Croix. You first cultural lesson is that a person born on St. Croix is called a Crucian whereas our world famous rum is marketed worldwide under the Cruzan trademark.

When I moved to St. Croix in 1980, I found the culture of St. Croix was not necessarily bad, it was just different from what Richard Schrader was exposed to and describes when growing up. From my perspective, it is now like our food; more Crucian Fusion than pure Crucian.

Since retiring as Warden of the Prison in 1985, he has kept busy by writing 20 books and selling them at shows and events on St. Croix. He sells and autographs his books at the Crucian Christmas Festival Food Fair, the Botanical Gardens Christmas Spoken Here, Whim Museum Starving Artists Day and the Agricultural Fair. You can also meet him at the vendor's market at the pier on cruise ship days.

You can support the important work of Richard A. Schrader, Sr. in preserving the knowledge of pure Crucian Culture for future generations by buying his books. They are available from him at the events mentioned above. They are also available at Under Cover Books in Gallows Bay.

Chapter 5

Before Your Trip - Decide What You Want to Do!!

For those of you in a hurry to start experiencing the wonderful island of St. Croix, you can start at home by visiting some lovely and informative websites.

The most complete calendars of events for visitors to St. Croix is available online. I suggest starting here to see if any special events are occurring while you are on island. They list pretty much everything from, which bands are playing to where the crab races are happening.
http://www.stcroixcalendar.com/

St. Croix Tourism has a beautiful listing of many of our more famous beaches but by no means is the list complete. However, you will get a general idea of the many fantastic beaches on the island starting with this description of over 30 different beaches. Like most long-term residents, I have been on all 30 of these beaches and many more and never had a bad time at the beach. If it rains go swimming, you will get wet either way. We rarely have lightening on St. Croix so you don't have to worry unless you see lightening or hear thunder. Then head to the safety of your car.
http://www.stcroixtourism.com/beaches.htm

Of course, on an overcast day you can take the rum distillery tours but be advised you should only do one per day and I generally prefer the afternoon tour for my libations. Most locals prefer the Cruzan Rum tour over the Captain Morgan tour but do both so you can join the debate.
http://www.gotostcroix.com/rum-distilleries/

For those interested in golf, we have two serious golf courses and one 9 hole fun course for hackers. If you have never played before, the 9 hole course might be just the place to start and no one back home will probably ever hear. What happens on St. Croix, we laugh about for three months and then move on to the next funny story.
http://www.gotostcroix.com/golfing/

There are plenty of tennis courts all over the island but it is advisable that you bring your own balls and rackets if you are even modestly serious about the game.

Upon arrival, you should pick up a copy of "St. Croix This Week," which is available on a rack immediately as you leave the TSA secure area at the airport and enter the baggage pick up and car rental areas. You can skim it while waiting for your car and bags.

The magazine and associated website tend to promote places who pay for advertising but you can also see the ads and make up your own mind as to what you want to do. They have a calendar of events, which is definitely worth checking. http://www.stcroixthisweek.com/

An even more complete calendar of entertainment and events can be found on line at St. Croix Calendar. Their listings are free so on some days you find too many things to choose from so you have to check carefully so you don't miss something you really want to do. This list deserves a second mention as it is updated weekly. http://www.stcroixcalendar.com/

Chapter 6

Things to Consider During Your Stay!

Shared St. Croix Experiences, Ranked by Relative Effort

Go to the Beach.

Many people who visit St. Croix have a fantastic vacation by just relaxing on our white sand beaches while sipping on a rum drink. However, there are also many other beaches and beach bars from East to West. Some of my favorites are Rainbow on the west end, which has a great sandy beach, some interesting snorkeling and a classic beach bar frequented by tourists and locals. Freedom City Surf Shop and Bar and Grill is another Beach Bar near a good beach in Frederiksted. It is north of the pier and south of Mahogany Road so lies between two good snorkeling areas.

Cane Bay on the north shore is another good swimming and snorkeling area and there is a delightful little Bar and Grill (Spratnet) at the west end of the beach. The crowd is a fun mixture of tourists, locals and snowbirds who think they are locals.

In the town of Christiansted, there is an open air restaurant on Hotel on the Cay. You pay a small fee to get there by the hotel boat, but the ride back is free. Nothing else is free as you pay for beach chairs etc. Nice clean beach, sandy bottom and spectacular feeling of wealth as you look at the town and the boats in the harbor.

Buster the Beer Drinking Pig

Ok, this is just plain silly, but it is a cult-like, shared St. Croix experience. The open air bar and restaurant was originally a domino club where George, the owner, made homemade rum called babash in his homemade pot still. Working men got together, played dominoes, ate food and made a lot of noise.

Dominoes is a game that is inclusive of everyone regardless of race, religion, creed, gender or age. Naturally, the group grew until it was difficult to describe the eclectic gathering as an exclusive club as everyone was welcome. Eventually, the government required George to get a license and to cut back on babash production.

George was also a farmer and raised pigs on his farm. Some of the men started pouring the leftover warm beer in the pigs' mouths and eventually, the pigs learned to jump up and take the can to drink on their own. Word of the beer drinking pigs spread throughout St. Croix. George and his wife started playing music on Sunday afternoon and residents and visitors started to flock to the bar to buy a beer and personally feed it to the pigs while getting their pictures taken.

The overwhelming popularity eventually led to rules to protect the safety of both the patrons and pigs. The rules are minimal as are the fees. It costs a dollar to go in and watch the show. If you want to feed the pigs, the beer is $2. The beer is nonalcoholic, because on busy days the pigs used to fill up and then go for a nap forgetting their responsibilities to put on a show. It is a great place to meet people and talk about St. Croix. I have never been there when there was not a mixed crowd of snowbirds, tourists and locals. There is even a song by fiddler Dick Solberg called "Buster the Beer Drinking Pig." George's wife Norma now runs the bar with a few helpers.

Snorkel for Free

There is always a place for fantastic snorkeling on St. Croix. The only issue is whether to bring your own snorkeling gear, buy a set at K-Mart after you arrive or rent it by the day. I will present a few snorkeling options and you can decide for yourself.

In winter, the winds and surf are generally from the northeast so the sea on the north side of the island is rough and the water turbulent but not always. If it is rough, you can head to the south shore or west to Frederiksted. In the summer, the opposite is true.

The Palms is one of my favorite starting places because there are 150 different species of marine life that occupy the reef in front of the hotel. When the water is calm and clear, it is a delightful place to spend some time. People who are guests of the hotel get all privileges and a guided tour of the reef, weather permitting. For those not staying at the hotel, they have a policy that allows very reasonable access through the front lobby. You have to have your own snorkeling equipment, which means you brought it with you or bought some at K-mart for about $30 per person.

Issac Bay & Jacks Bay

Many of our local people suggest that all tourists have to see Point Udall, which is America's most eastern point. The sun rises on Point Udall to start the new year, the new century and the new Millennium. As an aside the western most point is Point Udall in Guam. Hence, in the year 2000, the sun rose and set on American soil on Point Udall. There is not much to do at

Point Udall on either island.

We have our ugly sundial thing, which I have never figured how to tell time with. There is a trail from the parking area at Point Udall down to the actual point, which the young and foolish can attempt. There is nothing to do once you go down as the serious currents and sharp rocks preclude safely snorkeling or swimming. Last time I was that young and foolish was about 30 years ago, but I do remember that it was not that difficult a hike.

Issac Bay is a fantastic snorkeling area, especially when the sea is rough on the north shore. You have to bring your own snorkeling equipment with you. There is a parking area about 1/4 mile west of the turnaround at the point. The path starts at the west end of the parking area and is well developed all the way down to the beach. It ends with a set of wooden stairs that take you to the beach itself. About 100 yards west of the stairs, there is a lean-to that provides shade because this is pretty much always a sunny beach. Bring water, take pictures and leave only footprints.

It is only about 1/2 mile from the point to the beach and it is a beautiful pleasant walk along a well-maintained trail. For those who like to explore, the trail continues from the west end of Issac Bay over the hill that separates Issac Bay from Jack's Bay. Each beach of white sand is about 1 mile long and I rarely see any people when I hike in the area. The car rental companies recommend that you leave your valuables in your room and leave the car unlocked when you walk to the beach.

In a future section on visiting Buck Island, I describe the tour operators that take visitors to Buck Island. All provide basic instructions, provide snorkeling equipment and guarantee your safe return. However, if you would like more very low cost experiments with snorkeling and you don't have equipment, head to Frederiksted, where you can rent equipment at reasonable prices.

At the north side of Rainbow Beach, there is an eclectic underwater art exhibit proving conclusively that "one man's trash is another man's treasure." There are undulating plastic seahorses moved by the surf and current. There is a bicycle and other pieces that are out of context and attract your attention. Naturally, the stable objects are starting to attract sea life in a barren area of sandy bottom. On the following map, this area is **marked with an A**.

Map of West End Snorkeling Locations

Directions, go west to Frederiksted then proceed north through town on King Street or Strand Street to the road along the Coast. Keep the sea on your left and you can't get lost on the way to Rainbow Beach. There is a water-sports shop that offers all sorts of water activities. They also rent snorkeling equipment for a modest $10 for an hour or two depending on how busy they are. The people at the shop will tell you how to use the equipment and where to find the exhibit. On a sandy beach with no reef, an hour or two of snorkeling is more than enough.

For those who have their own equipment. Park in the parking lot for the bar, Rhythms at Rainbow. (Leave your valuables at home.) Cross the street and head to the beach by passing through the bar or going around it on the north (Right) side. Walk to the end of the beach, pass the first house and stop in front of the second house (sort of an orange color). Put on your equipment and swim due west towards the 4 buoys. Enjoy your swim.

South of Mahogany Road, point B on the map. This area contains a reef along the shore line that has coral reefs and grottoes full of fish. There is a beach bar ½ mile south of Mahogany Road, which is currently closed and unnamed. Park your car in the parking lot and head to the beach. Swim to the north (right turn). Stay as close to the shoreline as you feel comfortable as sometime the wave action will attempt to push you on the reef.

There are Grottoes with elk-horn coral and brain coral. The brain coral usually has colorful parasites, known as Christmas tree worms, Spirobranchus giganteus, growing on them. When you wave your hand, the Christmas tree, which contains both gills and mouth retreats into the protective brain coral host. Of course, this mindless endeavor harms neither the worm, the host nor you.

A more aggressive action while snorkeling at this location is to interact with black sea urchins, Diadema antillarum, in a somewhat more negative manner. In the simplest interaction, you poke the urchin with a dive knife, stick, piece of metal or crush it with a rock. The smaller fish immediately get the scent and flock to feed on the urchin flesh while ignoring you. If you ever step on a sea urchin and have no way to remove the spine, you will never feel remorse about feeding an urchin to the fish. (Hint; pour coke, lime juice or other food acids on the wound of a sea urchin to neutralize it and dissolve the spine.)

In a more aggressive manner, you can get really fresh sea urchin or uni in Japanese. A cute article on diving for, preparing and eating uni is found here. http://www.foodrepublic.com/2012/08/09/how-to-dive-for-sea-urchins-and-tips-for-eating-them/ As the article suggests, the only times I did this on St. Croix involved the consumption of alcohol.

Under the pier, point C on the map. Under the pier is a unique area of the coastal environment. The depth of the water goes from zero at the shoreline to over sixty feet deep and there are coral and marine life growing on the pilings that attract a variety of fish. The small fish come to eat the sea life growing on the pilings and the large fish come to eat the small fish. Occasionally barracuda and sharks show up to make a meal of the large fish. This is also the home to a sea horse colony.

Depending on how strong a swimmer you are, you can enter from the beach on either side of the pier. The shortest distance is to go to Stand street, climb over the sea wall and head north to the pier where there is a very small sandy area close to the pier.

The Freedom City Surf Shop rents snorkeling equipment for $25 for 24 hours. Thus, you can do the area around point B one afternoon and the pier the next morning when you are fresh. Be sure to tell them your intentions. They don't like to let the equipment go out overnight but they will let you use it the next morning. The fort by the pier is on one end of a long beach, the Freedom City Surf Shop is at the other end.

Night Snorkel

A night snorkel is completely different than the daytime event. The sea creatures are less intimidated by you and you can catch lobster and play with squid. You can also handle the octopus, but don't manhandle them, they will bite. You can do it on your own and the only additional gear you will need is an underwater LED light. Some people find it intimating so if you can find a guide at your hotel, this is an exciting adventure.

Night Snorkeling at the Palms

My daughter and niece playing with an octopus

Buck Island is a must!

There are several different charters to go to the Buck Island snorkeling tour and everybody has a favorite and is the expert - except me. I like them all and have never had a bad trip to the island underwater National Park and snorkeling trail. For those operators not in town, you must have a car unless you are both wealthy and patient enough to go by taxi. A cab from a hotel to Christiansted is not all that expensive and you can always find a cab back to your hotel. I will start with the ones I know and have personally enjoyed.

All tour operators provide snorkeling gear and instructions on how to use it. They also require everyone to use a flotation device and have personnel in the water to assist you if you get fatigued.

In Town:

Big Beard has a motor powered craft and a sailing catamaran. I have gone with them on the sailboat several times to both the half day to buck island and the beach BBQ - all you can eat and drink. For newcomers, a half day of snorkeling is a lot. For the young at heart, a full day of eating, drinking and swimming on the beach is fine.

Caribbean Sea Adventures has several boats including a glass bottom boat for those who think they may be afraid to leave the boat. This boat is ideal if you are in the company of very young or old people who are along for companionship and the boat ride. Every operator has swimmers capable of guiding and towing a non-swimmer wearing a life-vest through the trail, just ask.

Miles Sperber is one of several operators who came out of the Hotel industry and he learned at his mothers knee. His mom, Betty Sperber, was one of the best and most influential hoteliers in the seventies and eighties and single handedly helped create the St. Croix tourism product of her era. This business has just been sold to a new owner but Miles still works as a Captain taking people to Buck Island.

Jolly Roger I personally don't know about this group as I have simply never gone with them to Buck Island. They get very good reviews for the Buck Island Trip on Trip Adviser but so does everybody else.

Out of Town:

Buck Island Charters: To old timers like me, Captain Heinz is rather famous. He built and sailed his first ship the Teroro from Europe to St. Croix. He was initially a chef at the finest of restaurants before exclusively working to take visitors to Buck Island with old world charm and grace. He is now joined in the business by his son Captain Carl. He operates from the Green Key Marina, which means you need to drive yourself. However, Green Key marina is worth the visit. There is a pleasant poolside bar for lunch and dining at the Galleon Restaurant, a very romantic location. Be sure to ask for a window seat when you make reservations at the Galleon. The view is of healthy mangroves and expensive yachts. Live vicariously if you don't have a yacht of your own.

Llewellyn's Charter: Calypso recording artist Llewellyn Westerman is another ship's Captain who came out of the Hotel industry and has been sailing to Buck Island for over 50 years just like Captain Heinz. The St. Croix Yacht Club is nothing special but you know you will have had a special day when he rows you to his motor-less trimaran for your sail to Buck Island and back. Like all great calypsonians, he is a natural story teller so you should also be entertained. He still sings weekly at a funky little restaurant called Cheeseburgers in American Paradise, which is sort of a family hangout for local residents. It has a nice play area for children waiting for their food or for you to finish with the entertainment and your beverages.

All operators are monitored by the National Park Service and Coast Guard, therefore held to high standards.

Sunset Sail

In my mind, there is no such thing as a bad sunset cruise. If it's raining heavy, there won't be much of a sunset so we won't count days like that. Depending on the availability of qualified help, most boats that go to Buck island will offer a sunset sail. These offerings vary from year to year and even seasonally, so check the advertising in St. Croix This Week to see what is being offered. When you make reservations, ask whether the price includes drinks, appetizers or music.

Roseway

Perhaps my favorite sunset cruise is aboard the Roseway, which sails from Gallows Bay on the east side of Christiansted. This is a 90 year old wooden boat with a fascinating history that you can read about here. http://worldoceanschool.org/get-on-board/about-roseway

In brief, it was built by Harold Hathaway in 1925 along the lines of a Gloucester fishing schooner but was primarily used to race against the fishing fleet from Halifax, Nova Scotia and as a pleasure yacht. Of course, this is the Hathaway of the shirt company. Harold Hathaway used part of his fortune to keep his ship in pristine shape, which contributed to the long life of the vessel.

The Roseway was purchased by the Boston Pilots Association in December, 1941 and in the spring of 1942 it was outfitted with a .50-caliber machine gun and assigned to the navy. During World War II, all lights marking the coastal channels were turned off and it was up to the Pilots to guide ships through the minefields and anti-submarine netting protecting Boston harbor.

She continued to be used as a pilot boat until 1973 when the Roseway began her transformation to a Windjammer when she was bought by a group of Boston businessmen who rebuilt her below-decks to meet Coast Guard passenger-carrying requirements. She entered the tourist industry where she remained for almost 20 years until the operators went bankrupt and the bank repossessed the boat.

In September 2002, the bank donated Roseway to the World Ocean School to be used as their training school. At that time, she underwent a complete two year restoration. In 2006, the Roseway chose Boston as their summer home and St. Croix as their winter destination where they provide education programs for students and day sails for the public.

The sunset sails serve two purposes. First, they are an opportunity for World Ocean School to open the Roseway to the public, sharing her unique role as an active National Historic Landmark. Also, they serve as a source of revenue for the World Ocean School's ongoing educational programs. All proceeds support the programs of the World Ocean School.

Information on the sunset cruise follows their

St. Croix Sailing Schedule (November through March),
Pick-up and drop-off at the ferry dock in Gallows Bay, St. Croix.
Adults: $45
Seniors (65 and above): $35
Children (12 and under): $35
Reservations are required. Get your tickets right on line, or call 340-626-7877. You can get drink tickets as you enter the dock area.

Boarding begins 15 minutes prior to departure. Roseway sails rain or shine (it's an adventure). Drinks are available on board for purchase. It's not much fun to do a sunset sail in the rain, but when the seas are rough, the ride is fantastic. You get a little wet but what a thrill to be at sea with waves crashing over the side.

Lyric Sails

Like the Roseway, Lyric Sails has rapidly become an attraction for locals, tourists and snowbirds. Lyric Sails offers a romantic musical sailing trip at sunset off the west end of St. Croix. The charter company is located in the beautiful town of Frederiksted, St. Croix, US Virgin Islands. There is ample space on their 63-ft, custom built sailing catamaran,"Jolly Mon."

The night-time sails feature live music by local and visiting musicians, a cash bar and food catered by local restaurants. Enjoy the sail along the beautiful, calm West End shore of St. Croix. Live Music, cash bar, free rum punch and hors d'oeuvres. If you are very lucky, you may catch the famous green flash at sunset as the sun sinks below the horizon. The cost currently is $59 per person. Reservations are a must and you can book on line at http://lyricsails.com

Each month, they also offer slightly later and slightly more expensive, $75, night time sails. One is for the full moon cruise where you sail with the moonlit sea and enjoy the glittering waves. I have done this a couple of times and it is a fantastic experience.

The other special event is the new moon, stargazing event. This is a perfect time to enjoy the southern constellations, which are very different from those observed in the norther latitudes. When you are away from sunlight, city lights and moon light, you observe the stars as the Amerindians in the Caribbean did prior to Columbus. Yet, it is not completely dark. As your eyes adjust to the darkness, you will see in the distance breaking waves that glow with bio-luminescence.

To find the phase of the moon when you can sail at night, visit, http://www.timeanddate.com/moon/phases/us-virgin/christiansted

If you were not able to rent a car, your options are more limited but you can still book a sunset sail from Christiansted where two charter operators offer comparable packages. Both charge $35, both serve complementary rum punch, both leave the harbor and head west into the sunset, both offer a romantic evening sail that parallels the coast and allows you to see the beauty of St. Croix, both leave from the boardwalk in Christiansted and both get rave reviews on Trip Adviser.
http://www.jollyrogervi.com or http://www.bigbeards.com

Buy Hand Crafted Jewelry

You won't see it in any brochures or booklets, but Christiansted is the center for artisan custom jewelry manufacturing in the Virgin Islands. While the current revival started around 1960, silversmiths have been working in St. Croix for over 200 years. The industry was so advanced that Peter Bentzon, who was born in 1783 on St. Croix, learned his skills on the island and worked both in St. Croix and Philadelphia.

As a free black man from St. Croix, he was able to mark his work with his own stamp and became the only known free black silversmith during the time of slavery in America. He is the only Crucian to be included in the National Museum of African-American History & Culture in Washington DC.

Today, all segments of our community are working together to keep the jewelry design and manufacturing business alive.

Sonya's Ltd.

St. Croix still has a fairly large and very well respected tradition of Jewelry makers. Sonya is by far the originator of this cottage industry starting in 1964 with her Christiansted shop selling original designs handcrafted using 14K gold, sterling silver or both. Far and away, her most successful piece is the Crucian Hook Bracelet. This piece is so distinctively connected to St. Croix that people worldwide will stop you on the streets noting that you have a St. Croix connection. Of course, this has led to copycat pieces being sold and even counterfeits but you can still find the hook bracelet and her

original designs at Sonya's shop in Christiansted. The website for Sonya's store focuses on presenting the jewelry they produce.
http://sonyaltd.com/

Chris Hanley does a better job of presenting the achievements of Sonya Hough and the global significance of the St. Croix Hook Bracelet.
http://www.chrishanley.com/news-info/professional-services/st-croix-hook-bracelet/

Crucian Gold

Around 1970, Brian Bishop started developing his own skills as a jeweler by tying sailing knots in precious metal wire. He worked as a diver and when not diving, he sold his creations to friends, acquaintances and visitors to the island. In a short time, he opened his own shop and the business grew. It is still a family owned and operated business now in the second generation. Their web site does an excellent job of highlighting their employees, their designs, their jewelry and the island of St. Croix. Spend some time on this site before visiting them.
http://www.cruciangoldjewelry.com/

Nelthropp & Low

Rob Low purchased the Gold Shop in 1989 and relocated to the current location in Pan Am Pavilion in 1990. The Gold Shop was renamed Nelthropp & Low in 2005. They now have a full-service jewelers workshop where they do repairs, custom work and manufacturing of their own designs. They also work with customers to bring their own personal designs to reality. The website presents a nice selection of their work, gives a good history of the business and has a nice presentation on St. Croix.
http://nelthropp-low.com/

ib designs

Whealan Massicott is a relative newcomer to the Christiansted custom jewelry scene but is developing a good reputation because he has built a good team of designers. According to Whealan, "They share lots of laughter and creative good times. ib designs is feel good people making feel good jewelry." Nice website, which describes their creative process and showcases their designs.
http://www.ibdesignsvi.com/

Joyia Inspirational Jewelry

Joyia Jones and her husband Carlo Pedrini are the most recent to join the jewelry design, manufacturing and marketing community in Christiansted. Their business has grown quickly in popularity due to their personal touch. Their website is nice and they share family stories and the inspiration for their designs. Be sure to skim their blog and surf their designs.
http://www.joyiajewelry.com/

Our Street Vendors

St. Croix has a large population of people who are underemployed or underpaid. Many use their free time to make and sell crafts. Some are cooks, some are artists or woodworkers, and a few make jewelry. You will see these vendors at almost all our parades, festivals and by the pier on cruise ship days. Take some time and talk to them. Ask them, which product they made. Most will tell the truth. I have seen and purchased jewelry made from shells, seeds, beads and wood. These vendors are starting out just as our most successful jewelers did over 40 years ago.

Two of my friends who make jewelry also hold responsible jobs. They both started when underemployed but now continue because they enjoy the creativity and meeting people. Sylvia Smith has been active for years creating jewelry and marketing her creations to visitors. She recently took a position as Executive Director of the St. Croix Environmental Association but still intends to sell jewelry at Caribbean Night and many of our special events where vendors are encouraged. (1-340-220-5630)

Sheila Heuer operates as "Sandy Toes" and specializes in sea glass that she collects herself. I am sure if you find a special memory on the beach, she will be able to turn it into a tangible memory for you to take home. (1-340-277-5600)

Warning:

Most of the Christiansted designers mentioned in the first part of this section create a Crucian bracelet with their own signature closing mechanism. However, other shops sell low cost counterfeits, which are not locally made. Montesino International is the company that markets a line of bracelets under the name Caribbean Bracelet Company that are copies or in some cases exact duplicates of those originally designed and made in St. Croix.

They are attractive but they are made in the Dominican Republic so cannot be called a souvenir of St. Croix. The best that can be said about them is they give St. Croix full credit for designing the original bracelets while parroting all the legends and lore associated with the original St. Croix bracelets.

Listen to the Music

Music Lovers rejoice. St. Croix loves music, all music. We have music all year round at diverse locations. From Lyric sunset sail and Rainbow Beach in Frederiksted to Ziggy's and Castaways at the East End. Check the St. Croix Calendar at http://www.stcroixcalendar.com/

Restaurants with regularly scheduled music include Cheeseburgers, The Golden Rail, Above The Cliff, Blues' Backyard BBQ, Rowdy Joe's, Eat @ Cane Bay, Angry Nate's, Deep End Bar and Tavern 1844. Also, the restaurants at The Palms Hotel and The Buccaneer Hotel offer live entertainment.

Each town offers a monthly jazz concert and both are great. Sunset Jazz in Frederiksted begins at 6pm and the concert is free. It is every third Friday at the Frederiksted waterfront by Fort Frederik and the cruise ship pier.

If you want to sit and enjoy the concert, bring your own beach chairs or blanket. You can even bring you pets. Leave your coolers at home, food and beverages are sold by the civic organization that hosts the event to cover costs. Well attended by both residents and visitors.

Jazz In The Park at Christiansted Bandstand on the waterfront is between 5:30-7:30pm on the forth Friday of every month. Bring everything you need to be comfortable, blankets, beach chairs and coolers. Draws a nice crowd of visitors and residents. Just remember, this is a National Park so take everything with you when you go. Take home your memories, leave only footprints.

All of our special event are built around music so also check them out. The difference is that in this section, music is the entertainment. At our special events music is a supporting element of the overall attraction.

Interact with our Artists

I have been going to art shows and interacting with artists for almost 60 years so I find it easier than shopping for a new shirt or tie. Most of the galleries are in Christiansted but I believe there is at least one in Frederiksted on King Street.

While I am no longer active in buying paintings, I still love to look at art. I tend to gravitate towards paintings, which interact with my memories and help keep them alive.

When I went to the vendors market, at the cruise ship pier, I met Joffre George who was selling ceramic tile Hot Plates to protect your table, counters and tablecloths for only $10. The shape of the palm tree and the view of Buck Island in the picture above have special meaning for my family and you will find the meaning in silly things to do in Chapter 8.

It is definitely art, it gives me pleasure, it was very reasonable and I don't have to displace anything I have collected over the past 50 years, which fill my walls and have special meaning for me. So even though I am no longer actively in the market, I still love to visit galleries and art shows. There will always be exceptions in my life.

I have been to all of the following events, especially those that serve wine, which is almost all. Actually, since this is St. Croix, I know that they all do. If you go to Art Thursday, you may find a painting that will keep your memories of St. Croix alive. Minimally, you will enjoy the food and wine.

Art Thursday is the 3rd Thursday of every month. Artists open their galleries and studios from 5-8pm to share their talent and newest creative designs. Jewelers and other shops open late to join the festivities. You will enjoy live music and complimentary refreshments as you wander through the downtown shopping area of Christiansted. This is never boring as the exhibits are constantly changing.

Starving Artist Craft Fair at Whim Plantation is held twice each year in March and November. The Sunday after Thanksgiving is one of St. Croix's great bargains with an entry fee of only $5.00. The event is just in time to start your Christmas shopping while supporting local craft's people and artists. The March affair is also pleasant and inexpensive, but you may not be as motivated to buy presents.

Starving Artist Day at Whim has been held for over 20 years and features over 70 artists and vendors. In addition, local foods and drink are on sale and live entertainment is free. Go at your leisure. The event is open from 10 am until 4 pm and you can wander through the grounds surrounding the historic Whim Plantation. Plan on spending a few hours.

Caribbean Museum Center for the Arts promotes various events throughout the year and is always open on cruise ship days. Upstairs, in this colonial building, is a nice collection of local and Caribbean Artists. On the **Second Thursday** of each month, the Museum hosts a Happy hour from 5 to 6:30 pm featuring prominent artists, music and hor d'oeuvres. A cash bar is available for you to sip a drink while reviewing the art. Admission is a $5 donation.
https://www.facebook.com/cmcavi/events/

St. George Village Botanical Garden has traditionally hosted an art show called "Art in the Garden" using various formats from an open daytime program to an evening cocktail party with artists in attendance and their works on display. Traditionally held in March.
https://www.facebook.com/cmcavi/events/

Take a Horseback Ride

I am not really a fan of horseback riding and the last time I did it was 55 years ago when a friend and I rented two horses in Grand Teton National Park. We saw beautiful hills and valleys with deer, elk and bears. I actually liked it but simply not enough to do it again. I prefer the serenity of walking.

In general, all three of St. Croix's horseback operators get good reviews with a high percentage of very good to excellent ratings. Also, their ratings seem to be getting even better over time.

In reading the Trip Adviser Reviews, I notice that many people have horseback riding on the beach or in the sea on their personal bucket lists and were delighted with the experiences. Also, many who have gone horseback riding on other Caribbean Islands give St. Croix operators the absolute highest ratings.

Since I have no personal experience with any of the operators, I can only glean what I know from trip adviser and that is what I present here. But everybody who loved it, which is almost everyone for all of the trail rides, says that this is an absolute must for your vacation.

Crucian Cowgirls (http://www.cruzancowgirls.com/) receive the highest ratings on their West End rain forest and ruins ride, which ends on the beach. If you choose, you can ride your horse into the water or just ride the horse on the sandy beach. Everybody raves about the Crucian Cowgirls that lead the tour.

If you like the idea of riding a horse in the turquoise Caribbean Sea, then **Cowboy Steve of Equus Rides** (www.horsebackridingstcroix.com/) could be your choice. After a ride to a beautiful sugar mill ruin, you head to the beach and spend some time with your horse in the water. Steve gets high praise for his sincere personality and friendly ways but a few are critical of his showing up late while they worried that they were in the wrong place.

Paul and Jill's Equestrian Stables are the oldest established provider of trail rides in St. Croix and have the most interesting trails in the rain forest, which show the great biodiversity of St. Croix. (http://www.paulandjills.com/) Everyone is impressed with Jill's knowledge of the plants and history and are pleased by Paul's very pleasant nature. Some years ago, a few complaints were about Jill for poor customer relations, but that seems to have stopped. The trail ride ends with a small beach ride and you may get to canter for a short distance on the return to the stables.

Scuba Diving

Note: even if you have never been scuba diving you should still read this section.

Many operators offer a package for novices with training and an open water dive in the same day or spread over a couple of days. If you get certified in St. Croix, you can dive anywhere in the world.

While I do snorkel and love the close-by reefs of St. Croix, I have never gotten involved in off shore deeper water scuba diving. All of our dive shops are PADI certified and those with boats are regulated and inspected by the United States Coast Guard. Don't worry about misplacing your dive card. If you are PADI certified, they will find you in the online Database. I did dive fifty-five years ago and my niece learned to scuba dive in St. Croix so this is a fantastic place to start.

From what I understand, your dive experience around St. Croix will depend severely on the site you choose to visit. Unfortunately, this places you at the mercy of the weather and the operators who all have promoters and detractors. The issue is the operator has to dive everyday to earn a living and the weather is not always cooperative. They can always find a place for a decent dive but sometimes the turbulence or cloudy water of the more spectacular sites prevents diving on them.

Still among serious divers, St. Croix ranks among the best in the world. One dive operator from neighboring Puerto Rico brings a floating hotel over so serious divers from Puerto Rico can dive the Cane Bay Wall. This is the list of dive operators who have been in business for more than a couple of years:

Caribbean Sea Adventures
Located in Christiansted
Phone: 340-773-2628
www.caribbeanseaadventures.com

Cane Bay Dive Shop
located on the North Shore
Toll Free: 800-338-3843
Phone: 340-773-9913
Email: canebay@viaccess.net
http://www.canebayscuba.com

Dive Experience
Located in Christiansted
Toll Free: 800-235-9047
Phone: 340-773-3307
www.divexp.com

N2 The Blue
Located in Frederiksted and Salt River
Phone: 340-772-3483
Email: info@n2theblue.com
www.n2theblue.com

St. Croix Ultimate Bluewater Adventures, Inc.
Located in Christiansted
Toll Free: 877- 567-1367
Phone: 340- 773-5994
www.stcroixscuba.com

Sweet Bottom Dive
Located at Renaissance St. Croix Carambola Beach Resort
Phone: 340-778-3800
Email: info@sweetbottomdive.com
www.sweetbottomdive.com

Best List of Dive sites I could find; The list was developed by a passionate lover of diving on St. Croix who operates Airbnb rental rooms but is not a dive shop. If I were diving St. Croix for the first time, I would be tempted to stay with them just to learn about the best place to dive on any given day and who to go with.

http://www.villadawn.com/st_croix/scuba/st_croix_dive_sites.htm

Apparently, an exceptional dive location.

http://www.caribdiveguide.com/Cane_bay.htm

Sports Fishing

It is more than a little difficult for me to honestly discuss Sports fishing as I do not consider myself a fisherman. The picture above is what I refer to as honeymoon fishing where I charted the boat for my wife and I for a half day trip. I told the captain that I wanted to do a shoreline trip so we could observe the fantastic scenery along the Coast. Fishing along the shoreline almost guarantees failure, but that was not the purpose of this memorable boat ride. Well the Captain didn't really like my idea but he had a wedding to attend in the late afternoon and since I was paying the price for the half day, he consented to take us honeymoon fishing for our anniversary.

The Captain was bored so when he got about as far as we could go and return to port on time, he decided to swing by a homemade FAD (Fish Attracting Device) he had built to see if it was still functioning. Within seconds, we had three simultaneous strikes for fairly good sized dolphins.

I managed to land one, with his assistance, while he played the other two. Then I assisted him as he landed the other two. My wife took control of the boat under the Captain's guidance. Of course, our half day was long passed and when we returned to port, he still had to clean the fish before heading to the wedding reception as he had already missed the ceremony.

That was ten years ago and I haven't been fishing in Virgin Island waters since that time. However, I have a friend who invites himself along for every opportunity, which arises. He pays his share, drinks beer and hangs with a bunch of good people. He doesn't care if he catches fish or not he is along for a good time.

Fortunately, there is a web site for the Golden Hook Fishing Club, which runs several tournaments a year, presumably while the big fish are running. There is also a link to an article about the purpose and location of Government sponsored FADs in the vicinity of St. Croix.

Golden Hook Fishing Club http://fishstx.wixsite.com/fishstx

FADs http://stcroixsource.com/content/news/local-news/2016/03/08/dpnr-installs-buoys-attract-fish

If you consider yourself a fisherman, "Go To St. Croix" has done an excellent job of listing several Captains and boats that are available for charter. Even, if you are not a fisherman, you may as well try it on vacation to add to your memories of St. Croix.

Go To St. Croix http://www.gotostcroix.com/sport-fishing/

Fishing from shore is allowed and no license is required. You don't see many people doing it because many of the most desirable places are off limits especially in the East End Marine Park.

Perhaps the most utilized location is the Pier in Frederiksted. If you are interested, go down to the pier at night and watch what type of equipment is being used and what is being caught. While fish don't bite every night, there are enough big fish caught on a regular basis to encourage people to keep trying.

Currently, there is no license required to fish from shore. Inexpensive hand lines and equipment can be found at K-Mart. Regulations regarding recreational fishing can be found at Vinow.
http://www.vinow.com/general_usvi/fishing-guide/regulations/

Charter a Plane

A few years ago, my daughter and niece came to St. Croix for Christmas. Big presents are out of the question as they have to be transported back to the states. Initially, I was perplexed about what to give my niece and daughter as they are both successful and can shop for anything they want, which they occasionally do but neither is terribly extravagant.

At the time, a pilot was advertising heavily for introductory flying lessons and I recognized that neither would spend the money on themselves just to try flying but both would love it.

To make a long story short, they had quite an adventure and both loved it but not enough to continue with lessons. On the other hand, I found that unless you get addicted and want to be a pilot, chartering a plane for a tour or introductory flying lesson is relatively inexpensive. From their one hour flight, there have been ten years of stories telling everyone about it.

Ten years later, the cost of a charter tour or an introductory flying lesson is still in the reasonable range for a lifetime of memories. The dominant fixed based operator on St. Croix is Bohlke International Airways established in 1959 by Bill Bohlke Sr. The next in line of succession was Bill Bohlke Jr. with his wife Tuddy who ran it for many years. While they are still active in the business, their son, William Richard Bholke (Billy), runs the day to day operations.

There is only one way to get a picture of St. Croix like the one above and that is to get in a plane and fly. The island tour is described on the Bohlke web page as follows:

"Enjoy a red carpet welcome, complimentary champagne and gourmet snacks as you and your guests (up to three passengers total) embark upon a breathtaking scenic aerial tour on our modern four seater, Diamond DAA40 aircraft flown by one of our experienced pilots."

The St. Croix and Buck Island tour takes about 1 hour at a total cost of $350. If you are coming on a cruise ship, see if they can help you with a recommendation for a reliable taxi operator who will ensure your return to

the pier in Frederiksted. When compared to a taxi tour of the island at the same price for three people, this is a great bargain.
http://www.bohlke.com/scenic-aerial-tours

From the web site, in their "*one hour introduction to flying in a two seater, Diamond DA20, you can take the controls of the aircraft under the supervision of a certified flight instructor. Soar over turquoise waters spotting sea turtles and dolphins enjoying the unique beauty of our island's unspoiled beaches and rain forest from the air!*" The cost is only $200.00 including pilot, plane, fuel and airport fees so this does not appear to be a major profit center for the organization.
http://www.bohlke.com/thrill-flight-experience

Eat Local Foods

History of Crucian Fusion Cooking

West Indians love food, not only their own but favorable foods of every culture. Prior to 1928, the population was mostly the descendants of African Slaves who lived here from the Danish era starting in 1734. Starting in the America Era, 1917, the population shrunk as many residents became eligible to move to Denmark or the United States. The island became so depopulated and poor that President Hoover declared it the poorhouse of the Caribbean. Plantation owners suffering from a lack of local labor started importing workers from neighboring Puerto Rico introducing a strong Hispanic cultural influence.

Eventually, these workers saved money and started small grocery stores and restaurants. Since Hispanics were less than half the population, they served food and sold groceries that met the tastes of the entire population. Around 1965, there was a very strong industrialization of the island as an alumina processing plant was built and workers recruited from Jamaica.

Slightly later, the refinery was built and workers were recruited from the more industrialized islands including Trinidad, and Aruba. At the same time, Hotels were being built and many maids and taxi drivers came from almost every Caribbean Island. More restaurants and mobile food trucks popped up to feed the expanding population, which was working long hours and often seven days a week.

Almost every Caribbean Island was represented among the various restaurant owners but they all had to cook to the increasing complex taste of all islanders. Some wanted the traditional curried goat with white rice, others didn't care and wanted their curry with Hispanic style seasoned rice and beans.

At the same time each group introduced a new cooking style, they also introduced new fruits, vegetables, spices and grains, which completely changed cooking styles. More recently, health concerns have decreased the amount of salt, fat and pork in the diet.

For better or worse, fast foods have also come to the island and diets are still changing from the Cooking Channel and the Americanization of local television programming. Still Crucian Fusion cooking survives and all who live here gradually adapt to the local cuisine.

I first became food focused when I was trying to lose 100 pounds, which I did and to date, 6 years later, I have only regained 25. I first used the concept of Crucian Fusion on February 27, 2010 and in this case I was talking about the vegetable market and the gradual change towards more American style vegetables from the traditional self-preserved indigenous provisions that used to be so common because American vegetables need refrigeration. coffeepotcooking.wordpress.com/2010/02/27/st-croix-vegetable-market/

To start your journey into local foods:

Visit the Vegetable Market

I go to the vegetable market almost every Saturday and it is always a pleasant neighborhood event. It used to be that the vegetables were exclusively west Indian fare because St. Croix grew garden crops for it's West Indian population. In the hands of an older accomplished cooks, provisions are those starchy root crops that fill the belly and make a pound of pork or one small chicken feed eight. Sometimes I cook West Indian vegetables but am more inclined to do a Crucian-American fusion, which includes Latin influences as Crucian foods are already a fusion of Puerto Rico and Eastern Caribbean Foods. I also cook traditional Italian because of family influences.

Because the population of St. Croix is growing younger and more Americanized, there is a recently created interest in growing traditional

American vegetables. In winter, you can buy fresh cucumbers, (American) bell peppers, basil and parsley (all cultures use them) and American tomatoes. These are the best tomatoes outside fresh picked summer tomatoes in the middle Atlantic states. I also bought arugula, which I am not sure why it is grown here at all but it is part of the traditional Italian summer greens, and the fresh local variety is fantastic. I also brought a bag of scotch bonnet peppers, which are Carib Indian from South America in origin.

Really Fresh St. Croix Vegetables

The vegetable market is located on Northside Road (Rt. 75) just before it intersects with Centerline Road (Rt. 70). It is open on Saturday Mornings and the farmers start showing up about 5am to sell their produce. I usually go about 7 am and there is still a pretty good selection. By 11 am many farmers have left so choices are limited.

Visit our Cultural Celebrations

Throughout the year, there are several cultural activities centered around villages of wooden buildings where cooks prepare traditional foods that would all be recognized as Crucian regardless of what island they originated from. Various cooks offering soup might offer you Goat Water, Bullfoot Soup, Man Soup, Ox tail Soup, Red Bean Soup, Green Pea Soup or Yellow Pea Soup with molasses. Oh my Gosh, I almost forgot Kallaloo.

Kallaloo is a Caribbean dish that originated in Africa. It is typically made with amaranth leaves called Kallaloo of Callaloo in the West Indies, which grow wild. A combination with other greens is also used. When not available, spinach makes a very poor substitute. Kallaloo starts with a ham bone, with meat on it for stock and then fish, crabs, conch, lobster and salted pig's feet or pigtail are added. Okra is optionally used with care because poorly cooked Okra can be slimy. Traditionally, the soup is served on top of fungi, which is a cornmeal dumpling. Some of the best cooks make a lighter fungi by adding in some cooked Okra to the dumpling, which makes it moist and fluffy. Avoid vegetarian Kallaloo like the plague. It is a very weak imitation. Some islands skip the fish and meat and add coconut milk to the soup but I think the Crucian version is best.

Perhaps the biggest sellers at villages are either fried Parrot Fish and Johnny Cake or the humble dry fried Chicken Leg and Johnny Cake. Many Chefs offer a full holiday meal based on goat, ham, capon, turkey, chicken or Roast pork with side orders of seasoned rice and beans, fried ripe plantains, boiled green banana or sweet potato stuffing. It's hard for me to forget Puerto Rican Blood Pudding made from pork blood and rice or very rich and spicy Crucian Souse made from pig's feet as I like both of them.

Jimmy Carter visiting at Christmas village was so impressed with the local sweet potato stuffing, he asked for the recipe to take home with him. BTW sweet potato stuffing is not too tough to make and unbelievably it is made from white Irish potatoes as we call them in the Caribbean. I got my recipe from a lovely native Crucian woman with roots that go back to the Danish era who would generously share any recipe you liked with supreme accuracy. Other cooks always seem to forget one ingredient and assume if you are good enough, you will figure out the missing ingredient.

Off the top of my head, some of our most popular villages are:

Crucian Christmas Festival. The dates vary but last week in December, first week in January are the typical timing. For those who are not accustomed to large West Indian crowds, food and beverages are available starting about 6 pm and you can take them with you to go and eat in your room. Don't miss the parades, go early if you want a great seat, go late if you hate waiting for the parade to start. This will be covered in detail in Chapter 7.

The Agricultural Fair is huge and very well run. It is the only huge event on St. Croix where no alcohol is available and it is entirely a daytime event. If you go for lunch and stay all day, you will go home stuffed and very tired. No parade, hundreds of farmers, demonstrations and craft vendors.

The Dominican Republic Independence Celebration occurs the last week in February or early in March. Small Parade and Village. A day of National Pride and celebration of culture.

St. Patrick's Day Parade occurs on a Saturday March, Intermediate sized parade, some food vendors but no real food village like the ones mentioned above. A good excuse to drink beer all day with friends.

Eastern Caribbean Friendship Celebration Last week in August, First week in September. Food Village, Music, Traditional Dancers. No parade.

Puerto Rico-Virgin Islands Friendship Columbus Day has been Puerto Rican - Virgin Islands Friendship day for over 50 years. Parade, village and eclectic entertainment and food representing all cultures.

Our St. Patrick's Day Parade

Visit Local Restaurants

As mentioned above, our foods reflect our diverse cultural background. About 40% of the population speaks Spanish so you would expect Spanish influences in our foods. Then another 40% is descendant from Eastern Caribbean heritage and as you would expect, it has influenced our meals from roasted corn to stewed goat and the rich flavors of Asian Indian cooking transported from Trinidad. Without even consciously thinking about it, our local restaurants offer a Crucian Fusion Menu with almost every cultural reflected in their menus. I posted on the Crucian Fusion Cuisine of our local restaurants in a copyrighted article on August 10, 2010.

coffeepotcooking.wordpress.com/2010/08/10/puerto-rican-rice-and-pigeon-peas-arroz-con-gandules/

Part of the post follows:
"Years ago one very successful local restaurant in the Princess area, Oscars, offered Curry, pasta and meatballs, steak and baked potato, Arroz con Gandules, Rice and Red Beans, Stewed Goat, Conch in butter sauce, Liver and onions with mashed potatoes and more. Oscar is Swiss and has since retired to live the good life with his wife Cita on St. Croix. Oscar was not the only restaurateur engaged in **Crucian Fusion Cuisine**.

On the West End, **Villa Morales** opened just outside of Frederiksted about 65 yeas ago and Angie, the daughter of the founders, and her husband JT, run it to this day. They still run a catering service all week long but limit restaurant hours to Thursday through Saturday, 10 am to 10 pm. The seafood includes steamed red snapper, conch in butter sauce, shrimp, and lobster. They also offer stewed goat, BBQ ribs, roast goat and roast pork. For those without a sense of adventure, you can get a steak grilled to perfection. I have known Angie for more than 35 years and everything on the menu has been consistently excellent for that time. They bill themselves as providing local and Spanish cuisine or as I call it, **Crucian Fusion Cuisine**."

In St. Croix, Value and Service are extremely important for a population, which works too hard for too little money and many have to care for their children on their own. The easiest way to save time is to buy a big plate of food for a late lunch and then eat part of it again for dinner. Local restaurants, in my mind are those that offer full flavored food and large portions at reasonable prices.

This eliminates most fast food restaurants. If you find a bar with a few people relaxing and a steady stream of people coming and leaving with plastic trays in a plastic bag, you are at a local restaurant. There may be a large crowd of people eating at tables or perhaps even seated at the bar. However, the real identifier will be the constant stream of people picking up food to return to work. They will be represented by all socioeconomic groups and racial identities and the common factor will be the search for price, quantity and quality.

This definition includes all of the food groups that contribute to Crucian Fusion Cuisine and does not discriminate against the origin of any owners. The list below is incomplete, if you hear about a new restaurant, check it on Trip Adviser.

I have no doubt that a visitor would be welcome in any restaurant on St. Croix, so feel free to explore. Remember much of your experience with new foods depends on you. For instance, curry and roti use various meats and come with the bones in or bones out.

I love to eat with my fingers so love shrimp with a piece of tail shell, or chicken and goat with bones. My wife would only eat boneless chicken and shelled shrimp. She would never even conceive of eating a goat particularly after we raised a few for a couple of years. BTW, Roti is just curry in a white flour shell folded like a burrito. So if bones are an issue, ask before you order.

The following list is incomplete. My family has eaten at all of them. If anybody has a suggestion that meets the criteria of full flavor, large portions and reasonable prices, I will be happy to add the restaurant to the list. Also, some items may not be enjoyed by Americans. Goat is fantastic to me however it is prepared, yet many will refuse to even try it. I used to think King fish was dry but now I buy and cook it myself. Pot fish have great flavor and texture but many bones.

Grouper, snapper and dolphin or dorado are more compatible with American tastes. Don't confuse Dolphin with flipper; this is the fish called "very strong" in the Hawaiian language, mahimahi. Double check all restaurants on Trip Adviser to make sure nothing has changed but take severe critics with a grain of salt. It seems that some tourists are searching for local foods served in opulently decorated and air conditioned splendor, which will never occur.

The following list is presented in no particular order.

Villa Morales

Gets rave reviews on Trip Adviser for Food Quality, Service Atmosphere and Value. Many comments mention the owners in particular and the friendly family atmosphere they create.

Armstrong Ice Cream

This is a culinary institution in St. Croix. They have been making ice cream for over 100 years and are in the third generation of family ownership. They get rave reviews on Trip Adviser for their tropical fruit flavors but also have seasonal flavors, which sometimes get incorporated into their year-round menu. I love gooseberry all year round and also guavaberry at Christmas. My Daughter and Niece love banana and my granddaughters love mango. Don't be put off by the green color of the banana or the gooseberry seeds. The flavors are too good to pass up and there are normal American flavors for picky children. You can even sample before you purchase it. The also offer a basic breakfast and lunch. Everyone is amazed at the low prices for everything.

La Reine Chicken Shack Rotisserie - capacity 200 chickens per batch

La Reine Chicken Shack

Martha Stewart visited St. Croix in 2014 and raved about the La Reine Chicken Shack. Locals always talk about the food and highly recommend it. Good value and you are welcome to watch the chicken cooking on the extra large rotisserie. Mostly Puerto Rican Style Food.

Harvey's

Gets rave reviews on Trip Adviser but they stay in business serving locals; lunch only.

Kim's

Gets rave reviews on Trip Adviser but they stay in business serving mostly locals; lunch and dinner.

Singh's

Serves mostly West Indian Curry and Roti, inexpensive and filling. Not a fancy place but clean. Small outside eating area behind the shop next to the parking lot. Roti is an Asian Indian/West Indian fusion with complex delicious flavors.

Sprat Net Beach Bar

Comments on Trip Adviser have more superlatives than almost any other restaurant, but most reflect the atmosphere, drinks and the view. I think the food is generally good. Always ask Calvin what he is having for lunch because Calvin always eats his best food. I have known Calvin for almost twenty years and he has excelled in this venture. He has an eclectic crowd of locals, tourists and seasonal visitors (snowbirds).

Ace Roti

Mostly West Indian Curry and Roti inexpensive and filling. Not a fancy place but clean. Good value. Good Parking and large outside eating area.

Junie's Bar and Restaurant

Hard to find with mixed reviews. Many local customers who recognizes that the tables out front may not be bused quickly when they are swamped at lunch time. It offends some tourists that hard working locals who come everyday get preferential treatment over the limited tourist trade. Get over the attitude or go to McDonalds for equally bad service and worse food. The menu offers good local fare.

Cast Iron Pot

Good local food but service is "sometimeish." Some times the service is good and very friendly, sometimes it is slow and stressed, possibly because it recently opened. The food is always good but locals consider it pricey.

Chocolate's BBQ

All the food is ready and in a steam table that is refreshed often. Even if you arrive late and the steam table has been cleaned, they may have some leftovers in the kitchen, just ask. In the evening there is a local bar crowd but lunch is mostly food service.

El Sol

Gets mixed reviews on Trip Adviser but they stay in business serving locals lunch and dinner. Some friends only eat their steak. I like the Fried Chicken Chunks (Chicharrones De Pollo).

Island Cravez

Local food with some of the slowest service I have ever endured. Seems that the first time I went there, a public transit bus driver called ahead for a dozen meals or so just as we arrived. Of course, they could not prepare our food until the bus driver came, inspected his orders and left with his food. The food is good and reasonably priced. If you want to try it, pick up a menu when you first arrive then phone in your order for a late lunch on another day.

Honorable Mention

The restaurants mentioned above describe the complex world of our local foods. The food is heavily influenced by the heritage of the owners including the countries of Trinidad, Antigua, Dominica, St. Kitts, Nevis, Dominican Republic and Puerto Rico.

Centerline Bakery

This is strictly local food with no bar and not much seating area. People come for and leave with food and baked goods and take whatever they buy with them. My daughter always stops for the coconut drops. I have known the owner and his family for over 20 years and watched his lovely daughters grow up to be successes on their own without having to work as hard as a baker.

Blues Back Yard BBQ

When it comes to food, locals don't discriminate, especially if the food is full flavored and a good value. Go for lunch and a couple of drinks and watch the take-out business as locals flock to pick up their orders and return to work. From Trip Adviser; "Warm greeting as you enter... Daniel on the grill is very accommodating with personal preferences and the BBQ is out of this world good... This place is awesome. It's like a party in your neighbor's backyard. The best burger on the island. Super friendly staff." Check when they have live music, always good and no cover charge.

Kayak Salt River

If you want to enjoy all of the fine foods of St. Croix, you might want to plan on being active. I still stay physically active by working around my house and gardens, walking or engaging in something involving a waterfront activity.

Over the past 35 year, I have spent a vast amount of time in and on the sea either taking a sea soak, snorkeling or kayaking. A sea soak or sea bath is simply going to a sandy beach entering the sea and enjoying the company of good friends with perhaps a beer or drink and relaxing while the currents and waves massage away your worries. There is no equipment, no charges and no exercise required. If you go to the same public area every day, don't be surprised if locals strike up a conversation with you. No further explanation is necessary.

Snorkeling has been covered previously so that leads to a description of the joys of Kayaking.

Virgin Kayak Tours has a great web site, which is well worth visiting. They offer two kayak tours. Both are worth doing and very different. The bioluminescence tour is a nighttime kayaking adventure where you experience a living lagoon that radiates light when agitated. The historical tour covers the last 2000 years of human habitation at Salt River and starts at their museum of Amerindian artifacts at Cane Bay before relocating to Salt River for the actual Kayak tour. The cost for either tour is $50.

Brian and Jill are longtime residents who moved to St. Croix when we were at our lowest after Hurricane Hugo. They have been running the tours in Salt

River for about 20 years and I have been with them several times. Surf their site and you will delightfully learn about them and their family. Virgin Kayak has the longest history and the most excellent reviews on Trip Adviser.
https://www.virginkayaktours.com/home.html

Bush Tribe are relatively new and as of Fall 2016, they do not have much of a web presence. They get overwhelming rave reviews on Trip Adviser. You will have to contact them to find out what they offer and how much it costs.
http://www.bushtribe.com/index.html

Caribbean Adventure Tours offers two kayak tours. Both are worth doing and very different. The bioluminescence tour is a nighttime kayaking experience where you experience a living lagoon that radiates light when agitated. The historical tour covers the last 2000 years of human habitation at Salt River. The cost for either tour is $50.

They have an informative web site and receive mostly excellent reviews on Trip Adviser. Of the two people who rated them poor, one was an advanced kayaker who said it was too easy and one was a novice who said it was too hard. The tours seem to be just right.
http://stcroixkayak.com/kayak-tours/

Sea Thru Kayaks VI specializes in one option, bioluminescence. Their tour cost per person is $60 and they heavily promote their "Sea Thru" advantage. They receive mostly excellent reviews on trip adviser. One valid complaint is that it may not be dark enough unless you are close to the new moon. Unfortunately, on Trip adviser, there is an ongoing battle with a group tour where one canoe took on water in rough seas, still everyone came back safe. In my mind, an open kayak is not suitable for rough sea in the hands of an amateur.

I have been with them on a dark night where one of our party was scared to death and couldn't control the kayak on the calm dark night with no waves. Craig towed them the entire way so they could stay with their friends and watch the others play with the bioluminescent water. It is a very cool effect when you lift the water with your oar of pick water up with your hand and splash it on your legs.
http://www.seathrukayaksvi.com/

Thoughts on Kayaking and Safety

Over the years I have owned several Kayaks including Ocean Going singles and doubles and two open white water Kayaks. I have also used a double foot peddle Hobie Kayak and loved it. All are very different and have different handling features. To maximize your kayaking experience, you must learn a little about the equipment used on St. Croix.

The most common kayak used by the rental and tour companies are the one person (single) and two people (double) ocean going kayaks. These kayaks are designed for maximum safety in the deep waters of the open ocean, which you probably will never encounter on a standard tour. They are usually yellow in color for high visibility at sea, built wide for stability, are self-draining and virtually unsinkable.

They are usually propelled by using a standard kayak oar. It is not that hard to master and tour guides accompany you to make sure no person gets left behind. If you have never kayaked, going on a guided tour is an excellent place to start.

For those who are concerned about weak upper body strength, the foot driven ocean going kayaks used by Virgin Kayaks are a dream. In all the years I went kayaking with my wife in our double kayak, she never even took an oar along and just expected me to do all the work. She loved being at sea in the kayak but not punishing her upper body on a windy day. I loved and needed the workout, so we went out often when we lived in a condo next to the beach.

The very first time she got into a Hobie foot paddling kayak, she loved it. Her legs were in great shape and at the gym she could sustain a faster pace than I was comfortable with on the treadmill. On a windy day, I also learned to love the foot paddles because my legs are also stronger than my arms. On a calm day, I loved the oar because of the comforting steady workout. Either way, just tour Salt River.

I also loved my small open white water kayak because of the maneuverability and speed of the light weight boat. It was easy to control when going off shore from Cane Bay, even in the very deep water in that area. I was amazed and happy to find out that it handled well in small two to four foot swells.

However, on the way back to shore, there was a tailing sea as the surf broke over the stern and there was no way to avoid it. As waves broke over the rear of the kayak, the boat started to take on water. It rode lower in the water, which made it more vulnerable and eventually it sank. It took a lot of work to drag the sunken kayak full of water back to shore.

However, because of it's very light weight and the ease of transportation, I continued to use it in the bays along the south shore and never used it to challenge the surf again. In contrast, my double ocean going kayak, with two experienced kayakers, handled well in eight to ten foot swells both going and returning.

Once again, ocean going kayaks will never take on water in rough seas. You can flip them if not careful but they won't sink. Open kayaks will take on water and sink or appear to be sinking, which can be unnerving.

Stand Up Paddle Board – SUP

In 2005, Stand Up Paddle Boarding (SUP) was brought to Southern California from Hawaii by Rick Thomas and because it incorporates elements of strength training and aerobic exercise like CrossFit, it caught on instantly.

Paddle boarding delivers a full-body workout and has become a popular cross-training activity. People use paddle boards to paddle on surf and also on very calm rivers and lakes. There are no rules to block your enjoyment. You can even paddle sitting down and no one will kick sand in your face. This is not an elitist sport; it is for everyone who wants to get or stay fit. It has also been adapted to yoga exercise programs. And since you are standing up, you can enjoy unique views of everything from sea creatures to what's on the horizon. Fishermen in South America have been using the technique of standing up in their canoes for thousands of years.

Perhaps the first to understand the magnitude of this leisure activity was the US Coast Guard who classified SUP boards as vessels like canoes and kayaks in 2008. Regulations now require paddlers to wear a personal flotation device when paddling outside of the surf zone. The Outdoor Industry Association's annual survey of activities occurred three years later and counted about a million participants at the time.

Even before that first count of SUP participants, **Freedom City Surf Shop** had opened on the beach North of the Fort in Frederiksted in 2010. They describe the shop as a SUP Club and Training Center and offer lessons, rentals and sales. They are also the home of the Coconut Cup SUP Festival in April. They do not have much of a web presence but they are easy to find. Phone 340-642-2985 or 340-227-0682 They get very good reviews for everything.

In Christiansted, **St. Croix Water Sports** rents paddle boards and many other water crafts. They get very good reviews but I can't find out the specifics of what they offer prospective paddle boarders. They are located at Hotel on the Cay. Phone 340-773-7060

At Chenay Bay, east of Christiansted is **Paddlesurf St. Croix**. This bay is shallow and usually flat close to shore. They have a web presence that tells you everything you need to know about what they offer. Phone: 340-643-5824 Website: kitestcroix.com/sup/

All three organizations get great reviews on the experience and the personnel where they rented the equipment.

The **Barefoot Pirates** offer a very well received nighttime paddle board tour between April and October. I am not sure why the limitation, ask them. The boards are lit from the bottom and you can see the marine life very clearly. Their website is clear about all they offer. Phone 340-244-6599 Web www.barefootpirateadventures.com/paddle-board-tours.html

Hike St. Croix

Walking and hiking are a very natural part of my life. It is so natural, I can hardly tell the difference. For health reasons, I generally walk between 2 miles and 7 miles each morning. Sometimes I take pictures of unusual flowers or stop to explore ruins or a cemetery.

Each year, I also enjoy three challenging walks of twelve to twenty-six miles. Along the way I will pick and eat wild fruits and berries and usually stop for a couple of beers near the end when I recognize that I will not fail to finish. I walk along stream beds, trails and abandoned roads that can be treacherous if you miss a step. Some of these areas have no cell phone coverage, so I usually walk with others. However, when I get the urge, I will go alone.

If you are new to hiking in the tropics, please read the section on hiking safety. This also applies to walking safety, including extensive walking while shopping. The safest, easiest and most reasonable way to learn about Hiking in St. Croix is to join a hike organized by the St. Croix Hiking Association, www.stcroixhiking.org/ or the St. Croix Environmental Association, www.stcroixhiking.org

This following group photo was taken at the top of Mike's Hill on a hike to Estate Clairmount hosted by the St. Croix Hiking Association. This was a strenuous walk for almost everyone even though I believe it was described as moderately difficult. Generally speaking, the St. Croix Environmental Association Tours and Walks are easier than those coordinated by the St. Croix Hiking Association. Both groups offer a broad range of knowledgeable guides and both charge a very modest $10 for nonmembers.

Before taking a major strenuous hike, a good way to start getting used to the climate would be with a 2-3 mile walk or for the more athletic, a run along any of the following courses.

Judith's Fancy is a gated community in the vicinity of my home in St. John and the La Grande Princess area. Take Northshore Rode (Rt. 75) until you reach 751. Follow 751 to the gate at Judith's Fancy and Park outside the Gate. Go to the Gate House and sign in. Start Walking.

This path shown above includes a loop around Bacuba Road near the National Park. It is a little bit of a tough up-hill climb but if you skip the Bacuba loop you also miss the beautiful views of the Salt River National Park. If you are out of shape, it is easier to go straight from the gate and turn left onto Bacuba as the hills are less steep. This is a popular area for walkers and runners but remember people live here so keep the noise down, carry out your empty water bottles and no pets.

Altona Lagoon is a park east of Christiansted. You exit town on route 75 and after about a mile there is a ball field on the right and a strip mall on the left. Next on the left is Seaside Market and Sharkey's Bait Stand. Turn left past Sharkey's and go straight until the road veers to the left then turn right and go past the boat ramp and over the bridge. Park in the parking lot and start walking along the shoreline where there are picnic benches next to the harbor. Eventually the road loops around so Altona Lagoon is on your left and the Harbor on your right. Continue until you reach the parking lot. Pets are allowed and there is a child friendly playground on the right, just after you start your shoreline walk. Less traffic than Judith' Fancy.

Princess Walks

The Princess Community

Depending on which path you take, you can walk from 1 to 5 miles and not leave La Grande Princess. Starting from the Palms Parking lot, go to the end of the driveway and turn either direction at the end. It really is hard to get lost. The previous map shows a right hand turn and a loop to the west along the shore, which makes the total walk 3.1 miles. There is a group that walks from Pelican Cove Condominiums almost every day and will start their walk around 8 o'clock. Introduce yourself, ask to join the group and find out why our snowbirds love St. Croix.

Hiking on your own starting at the East End.

In my mind, the biggest difference between a walk and a hike is that there is nothing much you want to remember from a walk, you are doing it for exercise. A hike is to an area that has photo opportunities and there are many places to hike from East to West.

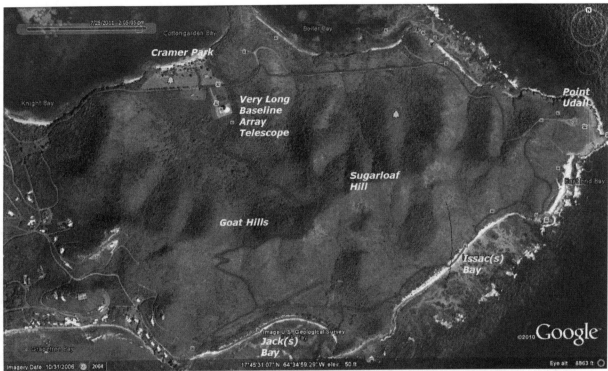

The East End is technically not one park but two. The north side of the East End is owned by the government of the Virgin Islands, the south side is owned and protected by the Nature Conservancy. However, for people walking the east end trails, there is no noticeable difference. This is the toughest of the three hikes that will be discussed.

This is a grueling 4 to 6 hour hike and covers five miles more or less so be prepared with water and energy bars. Start at Cramer's Park and head east until you find the dirt road to the top of Sugarloaf Hill. This is a steady 1 mile uphill walk at the sunny desert end of the island. It gets even steeper closer to the top where you get fantastic photos.

You leave the top and return to the saddle between Sugarloaf Hill and the Goat Hills range and start your descent to the beach. The trail comes to a "T" and one choice would be to turn left and head to Issac Bay. However, you would miss the other mile long pristine beach called Jack Bay. If you are tired, that would be the best choice as two miles of walking on the beach is tough and when you get to the Point Udall, the walk along the hot road is still 1.5 miles long to get back to your car. While this is a tough hike, it would be a shame to miss the pristine isolated beaches that will be protected by the Nature Conservancy forever.

Princess Nature Conservancy

For the easiest hike by far, you can return to the Princess area and explore the Nature Conservancy Headquarters for the Virgin Islands. The thing that makes this a hike is you go off the beaten path and explore the dense forest on the Conservancy property and observe a tropical forest regaining the ruins of a sugar plantation.

Entrance Sign

Road to Hospital and Great House

Bearded Ficus growing on Ruins

Sugar Mill to Crush Cane

Hospital Upstairs — Dungeon Downstairs

To make this a real hike, you can avoid all of the roads in princess. You can park in the Palms parking lot to the east of the Restaurant. As you make your way to the end of the driveway, keep going straight if you're feeling rustic. The road ends but there is a short path, which intersects with another path leading to a gravel road. Take this almost to the end and you will see the sign for the Nature Conservancy. The road will be closed with a gate on Saturday and Sunday.

Walk into the property on the road until you come to a clearing and a fork in the road. The sign on the right side says do not enter so this, of course, is where you enter. You will know you are on the right path as you meet a sign further up this path that says the trail starts there. Carefully follow the trail as it winds around among the ruins under the forest canopy. At the other end of the trail is the Great House and you can take an unguided tour of the second floor. The photographs on display are impressive when you see the magnitude of the rum factory and sugar cane fields. Remember, these buildings are working offices for the Nature Conservancy Group. If people are not busy, everybody will talk with you. But, keep in mind, everybody is working hard to save the planet so respect their efforts. You can return along the beach if you desire.

Hams Bluff is a historically significant place to visit with fantastic views. It was in this area that the runaway slaves congregated and formed a community. The Danish Colonial Government counted everybody included the runaway slaves and the estimated community population was ten percent of all the slaves on the island. This rugged area was also the staging area for the Maritime Maroons who escaped to Puerto Rico by boat or raft. As many as 300 enslaved Africans survived the journey over this hazardous deep channel in a quest for freedom.

It is also a location of the first American Naval Installation in St. Croix, a lighthouse acquired in 1915 prior to the start of World War I and the purchase of the Islands from the Danish Government.

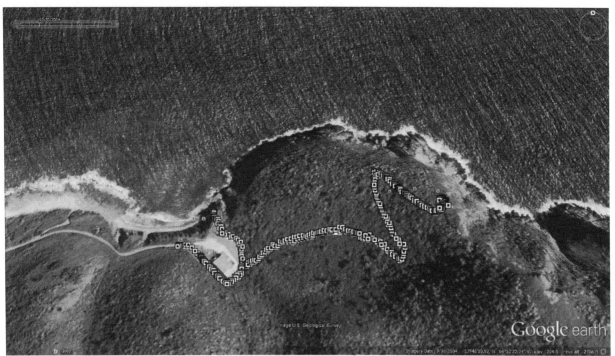

To get to the trail head, take Route 63 north of Frederiksted. Just before the road turns inland towards the hills, there is a beach house followed by a small bay. After that, watch carefully. The entry to the coast road is between two pillars, which are obscured by weeds part of the year. Take this rough road to the end. It will stop at a National Guard Complex. Park along the road but turn around first in case more people come to this popular hiking area and turning around becomes difficult.

To get to the main trail, which is an old graded road, walk around the complex in either direction. I prefer the safe inland way, many others prefer life on the edge. It's about the same distance either way. This is a short but but moderately strenuous uphill walk to the fantastic scenic overview.

These are my three favorite hikes for St. Croix based on beauty and photo opportunity. I usually grab a beer after a hot walk and the closest place for a drink on the East End is Ziggy's, the Palms is at the start and end of the Hike to the Nature Conservancy and Rainbow is closest to Hams Bluff. These also happen to be three of my favorite places to stop for a beer so that always works out well.

Maroon Hole — Suicide Rather Than Recapture

Unusual Cast Iron Light House

St. Thomas as Seen From Hams Bluff

East to Mikes Hill as Seen From Hams Bluff

Adventures

I have to admit, that the members of my immediate family and their children like a good adrenaline rush and so do I. Many of the previously mentioned adventures could have been included in this area but I didn't want to imply that water sports are dangerous. Besides, there is a great amount of tranquility in swimming, hiking, snorkeling, kayaking and walking to look for birds and flowers. My criteria for inclusion in this section is longevity of the business, good reviews and safety conscious in addition to providing the participant a few thrills.

Tan Tan Tours Picking up Cruise ship Passengers

Tan Tan Tours is the oldest cross country, tour on St. Croix and still has not lost the thrill of serving new customers. They have multiple Drivers including Wade the founder and Kendell his son. Their website is descriptive

and their prices are reasonable for what they offer. They even pick up individuals at the Cruise ship pier. Read more about their community service in the following section on visiting the Wills Bay Baths. Their Website is www.stxtantantours.com/tour_info.html
You can contact them at:
Office phone; 340.773.7041
Mobile; 340.473.6446 Kendell 340-277-0931
email; wave@stxtantantours.com

Another interesting way to see the hills, sea views and ruins of the west end is to go with **Gecko's Island Adventures** who offer ATV (All Terrine Vehicle) tours of the West End. Their website is informative except for a Navigation Bar that is set in a type font that is more unreadable than my handwriting. They also offer a Package with West End Water Sports to rent a Jet Ski on the Beach you return to and additional benefits. Phone 340-718-8820 Website:
Tour: www.geckosislandadventures.com/new%20ATV%20tours.html
Package: www.geckosislandadventures.com/new%202012%20package.html

West End Water Sports offers a variety of beach and water equipment for rent. My friend Ted, rented a jet ski and absolutely loved it. He has been on jet skis before but said that this was the first time he rented a jet ski that offered full power. Some complained on Trip Adviser that the machines were too powerful and difficult to mount for older people but Ted is 74 so go figure. For Caribbean People, age is just a number not a condition. They also have a Flyboard, which is a levitated balance platform. I find it fascinating to sit with a drink at Rainbow Beach Bar and watch young people standing on air with greater or lesser success. The various rental equipment rates can be found on their website.
www.wewatersports.com/rentals.html
Phone: 340-277-8295

Both the Jeep and ATV tours are exciting ways to see the west end of St. Croix but there are other parts of the island and other ways to do it. As mentioned earlier, you could Charter a plane for a complete tour of the island (pg. 38) or you could go hang gliding above Christiansted Harbor. I haven't done the Hang Gliding in Christiansted yet but I did it close to Kitty Hawk in North Carolina with my Daughter and Niece. It was fantastic and everybody loved.

Technically, the flight with **Hang Glide St. Croix** is considered a hang gliding lesson as the FAA only allows for the pilot and a student to ride the hang glider. Because it is a lesson, this is technically not a tour of Christiansted Harbor and Altona Lagoon, but you can't help but notice the beautiful views of St. Croix. They receive rave reviews on Trip Adviser and were recognized by the Luxury Travel Guide Awards for 2016 as the Unique Activity of the Year for all of the U.S. Virgin Islands.

On Trip Adviser, one person mentioned that the price was a little high and all I can say is that I paid more to take off and land at a drab airport in North Carolina. When I did my tandem flight, I thought it was worth every cent. If you ever dreamed that you could fly, hang gliding is the closest you will get to that experience. No engine noises and total serenity as you fly above the red-tailed hawks and sea birds while looking at the stunningly beautiful Christiansted Harbor.

There is a weight limit based on the area of the kite, which is set at 215 pounds. When I did it the limit was 205 and I had to drop 30 pounds so the kite would lift me off the ground. Their web site is easy to navigate and includes all you need to know to make your reservations.
flystcroix.com/
Phone 440-667-2377

After living in St. Croix for 36 years, I have come to accept that age is just a number and am very comfortable growing older. There is only one thing that has ever made me want to roll back the clock and that is **Kitesurfing**. The sport has been in America much longer than Stand Up Paddleboarding, but unlike SUP, it appears to take a more athletic nature just to get started. Then to be really good, it will take a lot of training and instructions to understand the winds as much as an Olympic Sailor, perfect the move of an Olympic Gymnast and understand the surf as much as a competitive surfer. I absolutely love to watch them, it is truly poetry in motion whether I watch them from 100 feet away or look down on the activity from my house, which is a mile away from the action.

I went Hang Gliding and whitewater rafting (class 4 rapids) for the first time when I was well into my sixties, however, kitesurfering is something to start when you are young and fit and then enjoy it for awhile. Unfortunately for me, this appears to be a high impact activity and I am not sure it would comfort my back, hips and knees. I am extremely happy for the fit young people who engage in it for their own enjoyment and mine.

Live vicariously by visiting the **KITE ST. CROIX** web pages.
kitestcroix.com/lessons/
Phone: 340-643-5824

Adventures come in different levels for different ages and personalities. For someone who has tried snorkeling but is a little afraid to move to the next level, Snookah Diving with **Aquaman Virgin Islands** might be an adventuresome next step. You breath through a tube, which allows you to go to the 20 foot level where there is more to see. They have a fantastic website, which has been dramatically improved over the past year and they get rave reviews on Trip Adviser. Website:
aquamanvi.com/Snuka1.html
Phone: 340-227-9828

For those who are afraid to try snorkeling because they are out of shape or not strong swimmers, **Mermaid Adventures** may be the solution to your fears and you can have a great experience seeing the beautiful world beneath the sea. You are pulled effortlessly through the water using a Sea Doo under water propulsion scooter like James Bond did in a couple of movies. Old timers may remember the Sea Hunt television program with Lloyd Bridges zipping around coral reefs being towed by a device called a scooter.

Mermaid Adventures offer a full-face style mask so you can breath naturally through your nose and mouth. You can also rent a Go-pro camera that is fitted to your mask so you can record everything you see and also prove to friends back home you really overcame your fears.

Moreover, they offer a tandem guided tour with very professional staff who stays with you the whole way. While I doubt that you would ever see a shark inside the reef, the Mermaids have thought of everything including revolutionary new Sharkbanz that harmlessly keeps sharks away. This well planned activity can open up a new world for those who have never tried snorkeling. Explore their website to learn about tour information and pricing
http://www.mermaidadventures.net/
Phone: 310-742-5015

Visit the Wills Bay Baths

   The stunningly beautiful Wills Bay Baths can be a treacherous destination. The winter months of 2015-2016 took their toll on tourists and locals alike. The sea and waves were particularly rough in December and January. Even the walk to the baths can be tough enough to cause heat related illnesses.

   Starting on December 20, seven young adults were forced against the rocks by large breaking waves. Battered and bruised, they had to hug the jagged rock to prevent being torn away by the rip tides. St. Croix Rescue was assisted by Tan Tan Tours to get to the scene, which takes about an hour after the initial call is received. The Rescue Squad treated three people at the scene but because of the nature of the injuries, they had to be carried out by stretcher (back boards) across rugged and slippery terrain to the waiting ambulance. All the rescue efforts took place after 5:15 pm, which is sunset in December so they had to do their rescue work in the dark.

Less than a week later, another woman was injured when a wave crashed into the baths slamming her against the jagged rocks. She had to walk out until her group got a cell phone signal and when notified, Tan Tan Tours took the Rescue Squad to the woman who was treated at the scene. She was fitted with a neck brace and driven by Tan Tan Tours to the waiting ambulance, which transported her to the Hospital. This time the rescue squad was spared the pain of taking the victim out on a stretcher in the dark.

At the time of these rescues, the St. Croix Rescue squad had responded to more than a dozen incidents involving divers and swimmers at the baths in just the prior three years.

In a news story, St. Croix Rescue Sgt. Liz Goggins is quoted as saying, "To the best of my knowledge, most of the people that have been killed or injured there had gone on their own, not with people well-versed with the hazards of the tide pools." But, Mother Nature does not have to respect the distinction between locals and tourists so anyone can be a victim.

The following April, two fishermen were hunting whelks in the vicinity of the real Annaly Bay just to the west of Wills Bay. One man fell ill and couldn't move so his friend had to abandon him for lack of cellphone service. He was lucky to be greeted by Tan Tan Tours and a group of tourists. The driver was able to contact his management and stayed to assess the situation and await the arrival of Tan Tan Tours with St. Croix Rescue personnel.

Because of the location and the treacherous hike to the top, the VI Fire Service, Police Department and EMT's from the Department assisted in the body recovery. It took almost three hours from the time of the initial heart attack until the body reached the ambulance to start the trip to the hospital. Once again this rescue effort was after dark.

No one is saying don't go, but use some common sense. If the waves are fiercely rolling into the baths stay on shore. Even better yet, go with a trained guide and there are a couple of choices. I have walked with Ras Lumumba Corriette who describes his hike to Annaly Bay [actually Wills Bay] as strenuous with a duration of 3.5-4 hours. Lumumba is knowledgeable, personable and safety conscious. I have walked with him and he is worth his money for someone who has never hiked the Northwest area of St. Croix. His advertised price is $60. Phone 340-772-4079, email ayaytours@gmail.com

A less strenuous way to go is with Tan Tan Tours. Their tour costs $100 and takes about 2.5 hours. You can contact them at:
Office phone; 340.773.7041
Mobile; 340.473.6446
email; wave@stxtantantours.com

Either way the cost will be a lot less than approximately $4000 that the rescue, ambulance ride and hospital visit will cost if you have a freak accident. Be safe, go with a professional guide and if he says it's too rough to enter the actual tide pools, you will still have the memories of some very unique and beautiful St. Croix terrain.

Bird Watching

When writing this book, I did a fair amount of research into tourist complaints but far and away the most unusual was from an alleged bird watcher who says there is very little avian activity on St. Croix. After finding out just how important St. Croix is to the global bird watching community, I just had to share this knowledge. I believe the comment from the bird watcher stems from the lack of knowledge about the very limited biodiversity of small islands.

The National Park service has controlled sixty to seventy- five percent of St. John since 1956 and prevented development of the land and deterioration of habitat since that time. The island was once connected to St.

Thomas and Puerto Rico so should have greater biodiversity than St. Croix but it doesn't. The Audubon Society works with local organizations to run their Christmas Bird Count on both St. John and St. Croix so actual facts support a greater avian diversity for St. Croix.

On well protected St. John, 31 people contributed 56 hours and managed to count 57 species. On St. Croix, 20 people working 45 hours managed to identify 70 species. The big difference is that from the east end to the west end, St. Croix has more wetlands and ponds and birds need the foods that these areas provide. Our dry forest rarely provide habitat for more than a few of the major species and you can't go bird watching around a hotel parking lot or at a shopping mall. You have to go to the wetlands or along rocky shorelines.

While some online lists suggest there might be over 250 different birds in the Virgin Islands most are rare or accidental avian visitors so a casual bird watcher will never see them. A personal blog of a seasonal birdwatcher claims a more modest achievement of finding 55 different birds, many of which are pictured on her site.
stxbirder.blogspot.com/

Two news stories on the Christmas Bird Count are on line. Both relate to the 2015-2016 Christmas Bird Count, which is the Sunday after Christmas.

stcroixsource.com/content/news/local-news/2015/12/28/audubon-christmas-bird-count-st-croix

stcroixsource.com/content/news/local-news/2016/01/08/annual-st-croix-bird-count-finds-75-different-species

The results of the count are available from the Audubon Society and St. Croix is divided into two districts. The east end and the rest. It would appear that there are a total of about 75 different species on St. Croix
netapp.audubon.org/CBCObservation/Historical/ResultsByCount.aspx#

On island, the St. Croix Environmental Association (stxenvironmental.org/) is one of the sponsors of the event. I checked their site and didn't find any information on the 2016 Christmas Bird Count, but if I had any interest in the topic I would contact them at stxenvironmental.org/about-us/.

I did notice on their calendar several events in December related to Bird Watching in December and January. On the January Tours, you will meet,

Toni Lance who is a Certified Falconer and Bird Rehabilitation Expert. On the tour of the St. Croix Avian Sanctuary, she will introduce you to the current residents of the Sanctuary including a pair of red-tailed hawks, peregrine falcon and American kestrels.

One of the important locations for the east end of St. Croix is the Great Pond, which is designated, a Birdlife International Important Bird Area. It is also the winter home for a Whimbrel named Hope.

Hope was originally captured on 19 May, 2009 in Virginia and fitted with a tracking device. A week later, she left Virginia and flew to the western shore of James Bay in Canada and rested for 3 weeks before flying to the MacKenzie River near Alaska. Next, she flew north across Alaska to the Beaufort Sea, where she rested for more than 2 weeks before flying back to Hudson Bay resting again for 3 weeks before leaving on a non-stop flight of more than 3,500 miles over the open Atlantic to St. Croix. Of course, as the original snowbird, Hope enjoyed her winter stay in St. Croix at Great Pond.

Hope wintered on St. Croix from 14 August 2009, until the evening of 9 April 2010 when she started her return to Virginia. Hope took less than two days to cover the 1660 mile trip averaging about 36 miles an hour. Hope left her residence on the Eastern Shore of Virginia after a 7 week rest and flew the 3149 mile journey to the Northwest Territories, Canada at a more leisurely pace. Including a stopover at Hudson Bay, the 12 day journey averaged only 11 miles per hour. In less than one year, Hope traveled more than 17,319 miles.

Hope was recaptured and the tracking device removed after providing information on the resting areas and migratory routes of the Whimbrel from St. Croix. www.ccbbirds.org/2010/03/05/hope-the-whimbrel-returns/

Sandy Point National Wildlife Refuge

The Great Pond at the east end is an important bird nesting area but remains unprotected while awaiting development. The salt pond on the west end is part of the Sandy Point National Wildlife Refuge and is another important bird watching area. The entire west end peninsula of the St. Croix is now managed as the Sandy Point National Wildlife Refuge, which was established in 1984 on 340 acres purchased from the West Indies Investment Company for the protection of nesting leatherback sea turtles.

As described in the US National Wildlife Refuges Comprehensive Conservation Plan, September 2010: "This is what makes Sandy Point geologically unique…. It contains the longest beach in the Virgin Islands because the beach is essentially an enormous sandy peninsula that wraps around the West End Salt Pond (and the western end of St. Croix). No other site like it exists on the island and its geologic formation is unique in the [Caribbean] region…. Maps dating back more than three centuries to 1667 show Sandy Point essentially the same as it is today." A guided tour of this is available from time to time through the St. Croix Environmental Association and the Hiking Association.

The refuge was originally established to protect important nesting habitat for endangered leatherback turtles, as well as threatened green and hawksbill turtles. This protected nesting habitat has allowed these species to make a dramatic local recovery. The refuge now has the largest nesting population of leatherbacks in the United States and boasts that it is also the best studied. From a very humble starting point in 1982 of 20 nesting females a year coming to St. Croix and producing 2000 hatchlings, the numbers have now grown more than tenfold with some annual variation. This has been a direct result of conservation and protection from man and mother nature.

In addition to the efforts with leatherback turtles, there have been similar successes with the less threatened Green and Hawksbill turtles. In addition, the Refuge is home to over 100 species of birds including some environmentally threatened species.

Visitors enter the Sandy Point National Refuge by the parking lot by the Visitors Center, just beyond the end of Route 66. If you plan on walking in, use this parking lot. The Visitors Center may not be open, but if the gate is open to the road, the refuge is open to the public.

Driving in the refuge is permitted. There is a second parking area at the end of the road in the vicinity of the Sandy Beach. However, using the road would defeat the purpose of bird watching because the birds are in the wetlands of the pond seeking food. If you walk the road to the point, you will see the salt pond, which is rich in marine life and the birds who are fishing for dinner.

When you reach the end, you can look for the Sandy Point Orchard in the bush next to the parking lot by the beach. Take your walk early in the day before it gets hot and look for birds in and around the pond.

Sandy Point Visitors Center | Westend Salt Pond at Sandy Point

The picture above is the profile of actor Morgan Freeman in the Shawshank Redemption and it was filmed at the place locals call Sandy Point Beach. It was just part of the story that it was Baja California, but in reality, it was filmed in St. Croix. Truly a place worth visiting.

Renew You Vows or Get Married

Renew your Vows

I eloped with my wife Dolores in 1966 and it was just the two of us in front of a Justice of the Peace. I now admit it might have been a little tacky. A year later, we had one of those big Italian weddings for hundreds of people identified as family and friends. It was really quite elegant. Since moving to St. Croix, I have been to dozens of weddings; some elegant, some casual and a few that were inelegant but never tacky. Some had live entertainment, others a DJ and some nothing at all, except for a raucous after party.

In 2009, my wife and I (pictured above) participated in a renewal of the vows around Mother's Day. The officiant was Captain John Macy who looked very impressive in his white Captain's outfit. The entertainment was equally impressive as the scheduled entertainers were Jamaican Reggie Artists, Yellowman and Beres Hammond. It was a great evening filled with good food, good friends, good music and a romantic setting.

This type of event is not regularly scheduled but if I were coming to St. Croix around Mother's Day or Valentine's Day, I would certainly check with my hotel to see if there was a scheduled event of if they could recommend an officiant for a personal ceremony. Captain Macy has since retired but there are other captains who look good in uniform and are registered wedding officiant.

Getting Married

"Go to St. Croix" has a page of information on how to get married on St. Croix here. http://www.gotostcroix.com/marriage-license

I know that it looks confusing, but hundreds of people come to St. Croix and get married every year. There are even intrepid people who arrive by cruise ship, after they accomplish almost everything before disembarking, and complete the process on the day they arrive to get married. Of course, I would guess that most hire the services of a wedding planner and "Go to St. Croix" has a list of them. http://www.gotostcroix.com/planners-officiants/

A wedding consultant might run anywhere from $500 up to $5000. Prices depend on the package. The basic wedding includes the location and the officiant. For more money, flowers, cake, photographer, champagne, limo, crystal champagne flutes, live music and more can be arranged. Most planners offer a free consultation. I am fairly certain that I will never be involved in planning a wedding again, but if I had to, I would start with the florist. Gloria Powell has had a life-long love affair with tropical flowers and along the way acquired professional schooling and apprenticeships. You can learn about Gloria at her website. http://antilleslilies.com/wedding-flowers/about-us/

I admit I am not much of a fan of pastel colors but naturally gravitate towards her bright tropical arrangements. Three of my personal favorites can be found on her web site as follows:
http://antilleslilies.com/wedding-flowers/2013/07/18/brynn-mike/

http://antlleslilies.com/wedding-flowers/2012/11/16/rovira-wedding/

http://antlleslilies.com/wedding-flowers/2012/10/23/anderson-wedding/

For those who prefer pastels, even in a tropical setting, you can browse a more complete selection at the following internet location.
http://antlleslilies.com/wedding-flowers/category/real-weddings/

I noticed in her three tropical weddings, Gloria worked with the same wedding planner so I had to check the site. One page gave a listing of mid-range prices and what you can expect at each price point. When compared to stateside prices, and considering that all of these options include dealing with the government paperwork, these prices look like bargains to me.
http://suncelebrations.com/elope-to-st-croix/

I was surprised to find a page devoted to cruise ship weddings, which deals with the complexity of a same day ceremony including transportation and the logistics of getting you back to the ship on time. Of course, you have to start planning with your coordinator when you start planning your cruise to St. Croix, probably a few weeks ahead of your arrival.
http://suncelebrations.com/st-croix-weddings-2/cruise-ship-weddings-port-of-st-croix/

While researching the sunset sailing portion of this guide, I noted that one of my favorites, the historic sailing ship Roseway, specifically mentions the potential for a marriage at sea among their chartering options.
http://worldoceanschool.org/chartering-roseway

"Elegant St. Croix Caribbean Weddings" by Denise Bennerson is now in its fifth year and growing. The magazine highlights local wedding planners, photographers, restaurants, bakers and venues for a St. Croix Wedding. There are online editions, which archives all their past articles about a wedding in Paradise. www.stcroixcaribbeanweddings.com

Take note that a marriage in St. Croix is a legally binding contract in every state in the nation. Same sex marriages are also allowed and recognized in the United States of America since June 26, 2015, when the United States Supreme Court ruled that state-level bans on same-sex marriage are unconstitutional.

Chapter 7

Attend Our Special Events

St. Croix has so many special events that I am bound to miss a few and make mistakes on the listings of others. My best advice is to check the magazine, **"St. Croix This Week,"** for their current calendar and to visit the website for www.stcroixcalendar.com/ You will sometimes find these two sources more informative and accurate than the websites describing the event. The reason is most of these events have been created by people who live here for our own amusement and often to raise funds for a good cause. The creators are not paid event organizers or web designers. Some events eventually get so crowded or expensive that professionals are hired to run them. Before that happens, seek out all of our special events and see what locals create to entertain themselves.

The first items on this list are commercial ventures in entertainment, shopping and extreme sports that are usually sponsored by businesses for commercial reasons but not always. A **Taste of St. Croix** started as a community fundraiser and it has grown to receive international acclaim. It is now so large that many locals skip it because of the crowds but it is still a very successful fundraiser for the St. Croix Community Foundation. However, most of our special events start out and stay community affairs but are still fun for everyone.

Celebrations We Hold to Entertain Tourists

Caribbean Night

Caribbean Night will be a night of romance and exotic memories for the whole family if you go with the right expectations about the dinner and the pricing for the evening. There are three venues for a Caribbean Night and all have their fans and detractors. The biggest complaint that I see for all three venues is that the food alone is not worth the total package price. Actually, that is a harsh assessment and logically not true.

Most good restaurants in our hotels and in the town of Christiansted offer dinner entrees starting in the high twenty dollar range with an occasional special of the day around $20. That price is per plate of food and includes only one meat. It's logical to assume that any buffet with multiple entrees will cost more because it is a wider selection and "all you can eat." That is always true for any buffet whether brunch, lunch or dinner.

My point of this discussion is that a fair price for all you can eat, chicken, ribs and fish, if cooked to perfection for you, should be about $40. Even if you sample all three, and only liked one entree and don't go back for seconds, a minimum price for dinner and desert in a nice restaurant would still be around $25. With this in mind, a rational human would find the price of $32 to $45 (depending on location) very reasonable especially when you find the show is a fantastic experience.

There are three hotel restaurants that offer a minimum of music, Moko Jumbies and Fire Dancers with an "all you can eat" dinner. Two get rave reviews for the show while the other gets panned for the food and boring entertainers. The two that get great reviews for the show use the same Moko Jumbies and Fire Dancers. The one at the Palms Resort is on Monday. The one at Carambola is on Friday. Visit one or visit both but don't miss out on this fantastic island experience. **Reservations are required at both.**

Caribbean Night at the Palms Resort

The Palms' Caribbean Night is the older of these two events and the one I visit the most. Their biggest advantage for me is that they have a huge parking lot close to the restaurant and they are easy to get to just off Northside Rd. (Rt. 75). This advantage will be important for anyone reluctant to drive on the left or who hates night driving. Also, for those not staying at the Palms Resort, the cab ride to Christiansted hotels is not that expensive.

The show is heavily geared to audience participation with entertainers who are truly local talent. The night starts, with singer and DJ Tony Romano who does a mix of Caribbean and Motown sounds. He mixes Calypso with a message with foolish Soca ballads and old time American favorites. Some of the more romantic couples start dancing right away without encouragement especially on a clear night with moonlight and stars. Tony starts with his DJ early but as the dinner starts, he is joined by the other members of his small band who play until the Moko Jumbies are ready about 7:30 pm.

When the highly acrobatic and energetic Moko Jumbies start to dance on stilts, Tony Romano kicks into high gear urging everyone on the inside dining area to come to the outside performance area, and dance with, photograph

and tip the Moko Jumbies. From toddlers at age two to hobblers at eighty, many choose to participate. Some people dance with them and some people dance between their legs. I have even seen a conga line form where everyone involved danced between their legs. The picture above shows my granddaughter happily dancing and dragging me under a Moko Jumbie's legs with a second Moko Jumbie dancer in the background.

Now that the crowd is electrified, the show transitions to a segment of classic and new wedding line dances that all the young people seem to know and enjoy. The crowd is led in dances such as the Wobble, Mambo No. 5, and the Electric Slide by three members of the wait staff, Kendell, Natalie and Cyd. On Trip Adviser, the tourists who dance are pleased that the restaurant staff is willing to dance with them towards the end of the night after they have worked hard all evening serving them as guests.

Kendell, who has worked as a professional in music videos, also acts as a caller so anyone not familiar with the dances can join the fun. I have enjoyed watching toddlers trying to keep up with the crowd and other people on the side just swaying to the rhythm and enjoying the energetic dancers up close.

There are two groups of fire dancers on St. Croix and while the older group might be slightly better than the newer one, you will still get excited as these energetic and athletic young people play with fire for your entertainment. They use hula hoops, rods, rings and ropes with burning torches attached. This is definitely not audience participation as they move the crowd away from their immediate dance area but everybody still loves the performance. Reservation are necessary, phone (340) 718-8920.

Price for the dinner and show is $32. Gratuity and drinks are extra.

Pirate's Buffet at Renaissance Carambola Beach Resort

Carambola's Caribbean Night is different in many ways but neither better or worse. They have their own Band and DJ who perform, also admirably. As mentioned, they have the same Moko Jumbies and fire dancing. The Moko Jumbies have been trained to interact with the crowd so they do. The fire dancers have been trained to avoid direct contact with visitors so they avoid hurting anybody. The first difference is the Moko Jumbies are introduced by the Manager of the Guardians of Culture Moko Jumbies, Willard John.

Willard is a St. Croix Educator and Historian and the producer of a DVD called **Mokolution: The Evolution of the Moko Jumbie,** which traces the cultural journey of Moko Jumbies from Africa to the West Indies where it survived in the Danish West Indies. Moko Jumbies were totally eradicated in most other Caribbean Islands where slavery existed before being reintroduced as a tourist attraction in the modern era. His talk gets good reviews on Trip Adviser and is considered a positive contribution to the night's entertainment.

What Carambola lacks, is the line dancing experience under the Caribbean Night that the Palms has. That would be hard to replicate because of individual effort by the restaurant staff and occasional participation by other staff members taking a break. Also, drink service at Carambola has been reported to be a little slow.

On the positive side, I consider the waterfront railing by the end of the pool one of the most romantic location on St. Croix. You can clearly hear the surf and watch the sea with your date. My visits to an event at Carambola has never been complete without kissing my date goodnight at this location and I simply can't understand why I have never been interrupted by others or even seen anyone trying to do the same thing.

Reservation are necessary, phone (340) 778-3800.

The price is $45 (not including gratuity and drinks), however that includes all you can eat King Crab Legs or shrimp. People still complain about the price of the Buffet and all I can say is get over it. If I were coming to St. Croix for a week with someone I loved and I wanted to be romantic, I would do both venues and have two different but unforgettable experiences.

Jump Up

Jump Up is a traditional street party that happens in downtown Christiansted four times per year. From the beautiful Christiansted Harbor to Company Street on the South and Queen Cross Street on the western side of downtown, the streets are closed to traffic and all shop and restaurants stay open for visitors and locals to enjoy the dining, shopping and entertainment.

There are street vendors, live bands and crowds of participants. You'll find local shops offering special sales. If you just want to grab your food and go, restaurants will be offering specials from their sidewalk locations and local food vendors are on the streets with traditional West Indian fast food like pates (empanadas), crispy fried chicken leg, johnny cakes and roti. Pates (empanadas) are dough stuffed with a flavorful meat and herb mix and fried. The moist fried dough does not fall apart when done correctly.

The entertainment includes the Moko Jumbies and sometimes a smaller fire dance performance. Overall, it is similar to a massive Caribbean Night but it is a lot harder to find seating. If you eat at a restaurant, it will probably cost you the same as the hotels charge for Caribbean Night. Regardless, if you eat at a restaurant or eat on the street to save money, just go and enjoy the music, the entertainers, the food and the shopping. It is a fantastic night.

There are four Jump Ups a year in Christiansted from 6-10pm For 2017, the Friday before Valentine's Day, February 10, 2017; the Friday before the Triathlon, April 28, 2017; and a Friday in late June or early July. This year the Summer Jump Up is June 30, 2017.

If you are lucky enough to be here for any of these dates, don't miss Jump Up. As to the market for the Summer Jump Up, the crowd is partially local, but a lot of people are starting to get married on St. Croix and as previously mentioned, the weather in June, July and August is a lot nicer than many beaches along the Atlantic Ocean.

West Walk

In Frederiksted, **West Walk** is a monthly event to benefit local businesses, support charitable causes and promote a renewed Frederiksted. On the second Saturday of each month, there is a footprint trail through town leading you to participating businesses including shops, restaurants and bars. Each business will host a shopping special, live music, and/or food or drink special. You can get souvenir cups at some stops. When you bring your cup to participating businesses, you get a discount. It's a wonderful way to see the town of Frederiksted before or after visiting some of the best beaches in the Caribbean at the West End of St. Croix.

The Caribbean Community Theater

CCT is a local community group that has been offering exceptionally good theater using local talent and producers for more than thirty years. Even more remarkable, the efforts use volunteers for actors, producers, set designers and builders. The group produces a minimum of 5 productions a year. Each play runs for about 3 weeks so there is a good chance you may be able to see one. Check their site on line and if you find something you may like, you can book on line. Book early, as many of their productions are sold out.
cct.vi/upcoming-schedule/

A Taste of St. Croix

In 2001, two restaurateurs, Kelly Odom and Katherine Pugliese got together and founded **"A Taste of St. Croix."** This was essentially a community event as it came in early April when there are only a few tourists around. "A Taste of St. Croix" served the dual purposes of highlighting the island's restaurants and raising funds for the St. Croix Community Foundation. The participating restaurants make a major contribution to the community by paying a registration fee and also providing enough food for judging and samples for 750 people.

Many also make a substantial investment in decorating their workstations where they serve the food hoping to win the coveted Best Presentation award. They often build stunning visual displays themed around food and wine. All they get in return is the chance for publicity if they win and bragging rights for a year. They also get a framed certificate identifying them as winners, which can be hung in their restaurant. Because of the high level of competition at the event, locals will recognize this as quite an achievement.

The first few years were successful in every way and the event started selling out the maximum 1000 tickets available. In recent years, tickets are sold out the same day they are offered on their website. To allow greater participation, a week of activities is organized with varying prices.

"A Taste of St. Croix" is now globally recognized as one of the finest food and wine events in the Caribbean and the week long celebration, the St. Croix Food and Wine Experience, was named by Forbes Traveler as one of the "top 10 international food and wine events."

A "Taste of St. Croix 2017" is April 6, 2017 between 6:00 pm and 10:00 pm. A ticket is $95, if you can find one. For more information, tasteofstcroix.com/

St. Croix Food & Wine Experience

To find more on the various events you can visit, http://stxfoodandwine.com/
However, nothing is yet available for the 2017 event. To get a good feel for last year's events during the April 7 – 10, 2017, **St. Croix Food & Wine Experience**, "Go to St. Croix" has a listing for last year's events describing them and costs for each event, which range between $50 and $1,000 per person.
http://www.gotostcroix.com/events/st-croix-food-and-wine-experience/

In 2016, tickets for the events were available online at http://stxfoodandwine.com/buy-tickets/

Annual Dine VI Culinary Week

The U.S. Virgin Island's annual restaurant week promotion is in the fall on

St. Croix. For 17 days in late October and early November, it is a celebration of our local restaurant scene and the culinary diversity of our island. Visitors and local foodies alike can indulge in cuisine inspired by traditional food and dishes made with locally sourced ingredients at special prix fixe menu offerings for a thee course meal including appetizer, main entree and dessert. You can dine at many of the island's best restaurants at $35, $45, and $55 excluding gratuity and drinks. There are also luncheon offerings at $15 and $20. For more information, visit dine.vi

Without a doubt, St. Croix is known as the culinary capital of the US Virgin Islands and everybody participates. There are about 30 restaurants participating in the program with about a third offering a traditional Caribbean lunch for a price of $15.

Big Events That Are Mostly Local, Everybody Else Welcome.

Crucian Christmas Festival

Crucian Christmas Festival is so big and so long that, it rates a separate description aside from the mention in the food section. The festival season lasts for about a month starting in mid December. While Christmas Day and the day after, Boxing Day, have always been big holidays in the Caribbean, the modern revival came in 1952, before tourism, industrialization and easy transportation to St. Croix. The early events were staged by civic minded individuals who wanted to bring joy to their communities over the Christmas Holidays.

There are certain words associated with the celebration, which have unique meanings. Our Celebration is called a Christmas **Festival** because the word Carnival is usually associated with a period of public festivities in the spring typically about 7 weeks before Easter. There are parades, music, dancing, food for sale, and the use of costumes and masquerade in the parades. Most of these activities center around a **Village** that is best described as a collection of temporary structures, which house, kitchens and bars for food and beverage service.

The Festival season kicks off with a **J'ouvert in Christiansted**. The word **J'ouvert** has been usurped from French Carnival activities because there is no other word to describe the event. J'ouvert is a large street party held during Carnivals throughout many Caribbean Nations. The party starts before dawn when a large crowd gathers to follow a band down the main street dancing and drinking along the way. The crowd then reaches a small and very temporary village for food and more dancing music and partying. Over the years, I have had fun attending several and my daughter and niece go, if they are in St. Croix for the season. I rarely go anymore as I forgot to mention that all this activity starts at dawn with the crowd starting to build at 5:30 am.

During the festival season, there are also several shows including **Calypso** and **Soca** Monarch Competitions where singer composers tell stories in song. Soca is similar to calypso, but the story is usually less socially conscious than calypso and the cadence is more uptempo. There are also beauty pageants to select Festival Royalty including a Queen, Prince and Princess.

The Festival Committee selects the dates for the parade such that the Parades fall on a Friday and Saturday before January 7th. The day of the Parade is also the last day of village. The opening is generally nine or ten days earlier.

Friday's Frederiksted parade is the **Children's Parade** and features schools and children's groups. There are costumes, baton twirlers, royalty, bands and more. It is usually less well attended than the Adult Parade, which is larger and more ornate and is on the following Saturday.

The **Adult Parade** in Frederiksted is stunningly beautiful. It is a costumed marvel of feathers, colors and choreographed dances. The following picture is of a friend who stopped and posed for me. Her outfit represents a portion of the Virgin Islands Flag. Most participants are very friendly to tourists with cameras and will usually stop to be photographed unless preforming at the grandstand for judging and viewing by the Governor and his guests.

The Wednesday before the parades is reserved for the **Food Fair** held by the clock tower at the fort in Frederiksted. This is another place to get good local food. Former President Jimmy Carter went and was so impressed that he even asked some cooks for their recipes. Yes, the rich and famous really do participate in our festivities.

Food Fair Wednesday starts early with **J'ouvert in Frederiksted** at 5:30 am. The tramp starts at the Post Office and ends at the Village before participants return to the Fort for the Food Fare. J'ouvert was previously described.

Crucian Christmas Festival, dates vary but the last week in December, first week in January are the typical timing. For those who are not accustomed to large West Indian crowds, food and beverages are available starting about 6 pm and you can take them with you to go and eat in your room. Don't miss the parades, go early if you want a great seat, go late if you hate waiting for the parade to start. Next to the Village, there are amusement rides for children, which open about dusk so bring your children. It is never crowded early in the evening.

While the show goes on every year including immediately following the devastation of Hurricane Hugo, the Festival Committee does not do well in updating their website. Also, since the magnitude of the festival depends on charitable and government funding, they often don't know how much they have to spend on entertainment. This year, 2016, seems to be an exception with the committee announcing big name bands from all over the Caribbean. It could almost be considered a Caribbean Music Festival.

Check out www.vicarnivalschedule.com/stcroix/ for a list of upcoming carnival related events.

St. Croix USVI AGRIFEST

The Agriculture and Food Fair for St. Croix is held over the Presidents Day weekend with a minimal daily charge of $6 for Adults, $4 for Seniors and $3 for Children. It is held on the VI government Agricultural Grounds just west of the University of the Virgin Islands on Centerline Road.

This typical county fair still has every thing I remember loving as a child. There is ice cream (Armstong is the best.), cotton candy, popcorn, a petting zoo, demonstrations, lots of entertainment and rides and plenty of local food and drinks. Their Facebook page claims to be the largest agricultural exposition in the territory and probably the largest in the Caribbean. Well over 20,000 attend each year including locals, tourists and snowbirds.

This event is by far the biggest event on St. Croix where no alcohol is available and everybody respects the tradition. In contrast, you can even get a drink at most funerals at the graveyard and many also respect that tradition.

Mardi Croix

This beach party and parade is our version of Mardi Gras and occurs on a Saturday several weeks before Easter.

Mardi Gras is a traditional associated with the Gulf States in America from Texas to Florida stemming from the Spanish and French Catholic settlers in these areas. The oldest Mardi Gras celebration, 1699, was in the Louisiana Bayou about 60 miles south of New Orleans. The next oldest was in 1702, which was in Mobile Alabama. New Orleans was a relative latecomer to the celebration with their first parade in 1837.

The Gulf Coast is not just famous for Mardi Gras, it is also home to a substantial number of oil refineries, which connects St. Croix to the region as many workers migrate between both areas depending on the availability of work. In 2002, a group of St. Croix residents decided that it was time for a Mardi Gras celebration on St. Croix. New Orleans native Dory Tiblier developed the idea and created an organization called **"Krewe de Croix,"** which is still going strong.

The group works hard all year to develop funds for their annual parade and Mardi Croix celebration at Cane Bay. They sponsor an eclectic list of many unusual free events, which are a lot of fun. The Kallaloo and Gumbo Cookoff (October) tests the skills of cooks who choose to make our local soup, Kallaloo, a mixture of meat, fish and greens and a simultaneous contest is run for New Orleans style Gumbo. There is a Rib Cookoff in September. They also have beard (January) and tattoo (March) contests, which are excuses to hang around a bar all afternoon and socialize. Slightly more interesting to me is the krewe de barkus where dogs are on parade (February) wearing various costumes. Since I love our local hot sauce, the one event I am most likely to attend is "Strand on Fire" in July, a hot sauce sampling and competition. About half these events occur in months where there are only a few tourists around but all are welcome.

Check the date and location on www.stcroixcalendar.com/ or www.facebook.com/Mardi-Croix-197969175138/
www.facebook.com/KreweDeCroix/

Their major event and reason for their existence is the **Mardi Croix Parade** on a Saturday, seven weeks before Easter. It is definitely a small but lively parade of costumed party people out for a good time. It takes place at Cane Bay Beach. Some spectators take to the water when there is a lapse in the continuity of the parade others sit and enjoy the food and beverages. Everyone has a great time. If you are in town, join the party. The following website has good pictures of the parade, so you can feel the fun of Mardi Gras in St. Croix.
www.stcroixtourism.com/st_croix_pictures/mardi_croix.htm

The next Mardi Croix is Saturday, February 25, 2017. The Parade starts at 12 pm but get there earlier if you want a spot on the beach. The party goes until it is over.

There are occasional Drag Racing and Horse racing events on St. Croix, which have fallen on hard times. Nothing appears to be regularly scheduled so I won't include them now. If you are a fan of either sport and you see an announcement for an event, feel free to go and enjoy our versions of these events.

Other Things We Do To Entertain Ourselves, Everyone Welcome!

The Guavaberry Festival

Kicking off the local Christmas Season, there is a relatively new event, **The Guavaberry Festival,** which takes place at **St. George Village Botanical Garden.** Entertainment includes Stanley & the Ten Sleepless Knights, Ay-Ay Cultural Dance Company and Guardians of Culture Moko Jumbies. It takes place from 11am-6pm but arrive around noon if you want to catch the entertainment. Next year, it will be on Sunday November 18, 2017. While this event is relatively new, I would be very surprised if it hasn't been done before in earlier decades. Their first event was rained out last year but they still called 2016 the second annual. This is old time original Crucian Culture from a more close knit community years ago.

Stanley and his musicians play a unique form of Virgin Islands music called quelbe. It went out of vogue for awhile as the lyrics of quelbe songs often contained sexual innuendo and double entendre, telling stories of clandestine sexual trysts and other lewd behavior. Despite these reservations, in 2003, the Virgin Islands legislature passed a bill officially making quelbe "the vocal and instrumental style of the Virgin Islands." Early in 2016, The Smithsonian Institution released a quelbe music album by Stanley and the Ten Sleepless Knights. The dance, which accompanies quelbe music, is called quadrille and is sort of a precursor to square dancing. It is beautiful to watch and almost impossible to do.

In the old days when people listened and danced to quelbe, raw rum and sugar were abundant and guavaberries grew only in the vicinity of St. Croix. If you mixed the harsh raw rum with sugar and the flavorful fruit, you got a much better drink. Today, people make Guavaberry Rum with the best of ingredients so it is a nice mellow drink. The limiting factor is the scarcity of guvaberries. I always have a few bottles stashed for Christmas and everybody in my family loves it.

This is a delightful afternoon of food, music and guavaberry rum. It is organized by Stanley and his supporters as a fundraiser for their scholarship fund. The event takes place between 11 am and 6 pm. Information is available from St. George Village Botanical Garden Phone: (340) 692-2874. Admission for adults is $6, children less.

Coconut Festival

The St. Croix Farmers in Action is a group of farmers dedicated to expanding farming activities and markets on St. Croix. They are active in a wide variety of events and November was their first Coconut Festival. They had food, crafts, music and more. They held demonstrations on extracting oil from the nut and also on preparing gluten free coconut flour. You could learn the secrets of making your own coconut cream. Many vendors have various coconut products on sale from tarts and cookies to coconut water and Coquito. The group intends to hold this event twice a year in November and April so check the St. Croix calendars. There is no admission charge.

Thanksgiving in St. Croix starts then traditional American Christmas Shopping Season and on Friday there is a **Jump Up,** which was discussed under regularly scheduled event.

Starving Artists Day at Whim Museum

The Sunday after Thanksgiving is the annual **Starving Artists Day at Whim Museum** from 10am-4pm. The Starving Artist Craft Fair is a pleasant afternoon for gift buyers and art lovers featuring locally hand-crafted items, delicious local foods and drinks and live entertainment.

You can spend the day wandering through the historic Whim Plantation grounds photographing the plantation ruins while focusing on the potential for wonderful and unique Christmas presents purchased directly from local craftspeople and artists. Admission is only $5.00 with children under 12 free.

Christmas Spoken Here

Christmas Spoken Here is another Craft & Food Fair held on the first Sunday in December and runs from 11 am to 5 pm. The event at the **St George Village Botanical Gardens** featuring local food, drinks and hand-crafted items made locally on St. Croix. In addition to shopping for our locally produced crafts, you can wander the beautiful Gardens and visit the marvelously decorated Christmas Tree in the Great Hall where a choir will be preforming Christmas Carols.

The Annual Cruzan Latin Caribbean Pig Roast Festival

Also on the first weekend in December will be **The Annual Cruzan Latin Caribbean Pig Roast Festival.** This year, 2016, will be the 12th event and will feature the band, Unltd Sounds, for the Festival del Lechon at Canegata Ball Park beginning at 10am. This is an all day affair with the pig roasters starting early in the morning and roasting their pigs on homemade rotisseries that can easily handle a 300 pound pig.

Many of the contestants will involve a family affair and roast as many as 6 or 7 pigs confidant that they will sell out based on their reputation. Some roasters will include a pig and a turkey on each "stick." Each group will use their own proprietary and secret spice blend and many will have gone to the trouble of making their own charcoal out of the sweet woods of St. Croix. Stop by early on your way to the beach to watch the pig roaster set up. Come back in the afternoon to eat your fill and listen to the Latin music of Unltd Sounds. Check the date and location on www.stcroixcalendar.com/

The St. Croix Christmas Boat Parade

The Boat Parade is Saturday December 10, 2016. **The St. Croix Christmas Boat Parade** is the largest boat parade in the Caribbean drawing out the entire community including visitors. The day's events start early with entertainment on the boardwalk at Noon and a pet parade at 1 pm on King Street. Santa shows up sometime during the day and wanders the boardwalk. The Boat Parade starts at 6pm with fireworks immediately following. Parade and activities are free, refreshments and food are extra.

This event simply does not photograph well in Black and White. Professional Photographer, Alda Anduze, suggested I use a couple of her prints, but I couldn't do justice to the detailed fantastic work of the boat owners. The best I can do is to send you to her facebook album. https://www.facebook.com/STXBoatParade/photos/?
Check the date and activities on www.stcroixcalendar.com/

The La Reine Chicken Shack Coquito Festival

The La Reine Chicken Shack Coquito Festival will be on December 17, 2016 and is usually in the middle of December. Just as Guavaberry Rum is part of the Oldest Crucian Traditions, Coquito was brought to the island by the Puerto Rican workers who came to work in St. Croix after the American acquisition in 1917. The drink is similar to eggnog but usually made without eggs. It is a holiday tradition for Christmas and the New Year, which has been adapted by every cultural group on the island. It is generally made with rum, coconut milk, sweet condensed milk, vanilla, cinnamon, nutmeg, and cloves. The art of winning the contest is to change the recipe enough to stand out but not enough to violate the traditional taste. I also keep a bottle of Coquito around for the holidays.

One happening, which is fairly unique, is that Santa arrives on a fire truck with lights flashing and sirens and horns blasting. Santa is a substitute for the Three Kings who won't arrive until January 6th. The fire truck is used as there is no snow or reindeer on St. Croix and the reindeer are resting for their big night. Entertainment will be by Unltd Sounds but varies from year to year. Vendors provide samples and the La Reine Chicken Shack's famous slow roasted chicken will be on sale.

Christmas Festival, December-January (see above)

The SEAstock Annual Beach Party & Fundraiser

The SEAstock Annual Beach Party & Fundraiser is generally held in January at Chenay Bay Beach Resort. The **St. Croix Environmental Association** hosts the annual beach party and fundraiser. The location is adjacent to a bird Sanctuary they administer and the offshore island in Chenay Bay is a federally protected Bird Sanctuary. Kids and family activities include tie-dying, a snorkel clinic and a beach scavenger hunt from 4-6 pm. Music and dancing from 6- 10 pm. Adult admission in the past has been $20.

Annual Johnny Cake Eating Contest

Ziggy's Bar, which has been previously mentioned, is more properly called **Ziggy's Island Market & Gas Station,** which also has a deli and outside eating and drinking area. The business holds various events for the east end residents and at the end of January they have their **Annual Johnny Cake Eating Contest,** which benefits the Boys & Girls Club of St. Croix and the St. Croix Foundation.

For those who don't know, Johnny Cakes are just fried dough that should be cooked all the way through and still remain a golden brown color while not greasy or burnt. Who would ever believe that you took time away from a beach vacation to eat fried bread, drink beer and play corn-hole at a gas station. But this is a great opportunity to meet East End Residents. If you can't make the east end contest, you can get a Johnny Cake at almost every event and local restaurant on St. Croix but you will miss all the fun.

Agricultural Fair, Presidents Day Weekend (see above)

Mardi Croix, Prior to Easter (see above)

Animal Jam

Animal Jam, End of May. $10 for Adults, $5 for13-17yrs and free for 12 and under. Animal Jam is a Beach Party with live music to benefit the non-profits on St. Croix who work hard to support abandoned pets and promote animal welfare. Bring out the entire family for a fun day of games, live music and learn more about animal welfare on St. Croix

Mango Melee at St. George Village Botanical Garden

Mango Melee at St. George Village Botanical Garden, Mid July From 12:00 pm to 6:00 pm. This is a great social event for everyone on island in July. Dates will vary depending on the mango crop. Local cooks compete to sell various mango based treats and local foods. There are also craft vendors presenting artwork, jewelry, clothes and more. Activities include children's and adults' mango eating contests. The Mango Dis, Mango Dat food competition will give local chefs a chance to show off their culinary skills and win bragging rights for the year.

Oktoberfest

Oktoberfest, 2016 with Santa Cruz Brass Band playing oompah music at Ziggy's Island Market and Gas Station from 4-11pm. In the January Johnny Cake celebration at Ziggy's, the focus is on the fried dough and the beer washes it down. At the Oktoberfest, the focus is on the imported kegs of beer and the food, including Johnny Cakes, keeps you satisfied. Check the October date and activities on www.stcroixcalendar.com/

Extreme Sports

Dolphin's Sea Swim

Because our weather is almost perfect all year long, many major events are offered during the year, especially in Winter. The first event of the year is the **Dolphin's Sea Swim,** which is scheduled for Sunday, January 8 in 2017. This Open Water Swim Race starts with a blow from a conch shell and a jump off the Frederiksted Pier, and finishes at Rainbow Beach (about 1 mile). Along the way, kayakers parallel the swimmers to ensure that nobody veers off course losing time.

The website for this event shows pictures of the college teams that participate on an annual basis but individual swimmers are encouraged if you don't mind being beaten by young people. As a consolation, your $45 registration fee includes a Goody Bag, T-Shirt and Lunch. There is also a category for people who want to register for the swim and use snorkeling gear. Before December 1, your registration fee is only $30. Their website is http://www.stcroixdolphins.org/events-donate.html

The St. Croix Scenic 50

The St. Croix Scenic 50 on January 22, 2017, starts at 5:00 am. For those not familiar with the course, this is a difficult endurance marathon. A few years back I took my niece and daughter for an 18 mile hike along the toughest part of the course. When we got to the end my daughter declared that the hike was proof that she and her cousin would follow me anywhere but never ever ask them to do it again.

People doing the 50 mile marathon get to cover this section of the course twice and some of them even take less time than the three of us took to cover the 18 miles. It is tough, but I know my daughter, my niece and myself accomplished something that few people will ever even attempt. There is also a 50K course, which is almost as tough but just a little shorter. For details and to register go to: www.stcroix50.com

Annual Coconut SUP

The **Freedom City Surf Shop** and Stand Up Paddleboarding (SUP) are covered separately but the shop is also host to the Annual Coconut SUP held in early April. There are two days of races, demos, clinics, music and entertainment. Competitors paddle a 5km Open, 10km Long Course and 12km Elite Downwinder with $10,000 in Cash Prizes. If you are not familiar with SUP, this is a good place to watch the activity. There is no admission for spectators. Check one of the St. Croix calendars for dates in 2017 or if really interested, phone 340-642-2985 or 340-227-0682

The St. Croix 70.3 Ironman Triathlon

The St. Croix 70.3 Ironman aka Beauty & the Beast will be held this year on May 7, 2017. The event started in 1988 and my son competed in that race. He finished in something like 4 hours but he was 16 at the time and I believe this was his first Triathlon. The race is known around the world as "Beauty and the Beast" because it is one of the most beautiful and toughest races in the triathlon circuit. It gets a fair amount of television coverage world-wide because both the island and the racers are the stars. Can't find a website for the event but if you are a triathlete, you already know how to find them.

The St. Croix Coral Reef Swim

The St. Croix Coral Reef Swim for 2016 is on November 6. The swim attracts enthusiastic amateurs and professional gold medal winning Olympians. The swim parallels the shoreline on the relatively undeveloped north shore. Most swimmers never get to enjoy the gorgeous scenery except for the boat ride out to the start of the open water ocean swim race from Buck Island National Reef Monument to the Buccaneer Resort's Mermaid Beach. The kayakers who monitor the swimmers have a much more enjoyable day as the wind and current assist them along the course. The race includes 1-mile, 2-mile and the full 5-mile courses. For more information and to register visit: **swimrace.com**

St. Croix Marathon and Half Marathon

The Virgin Islands Pace Runners have been organizing races on St. Croix

for 38 years and they make it easy to participate inviting walkers, joggers and runners to their various events. Races and walks start at 1 mile long and many are under 5 miles. On the second Sunday in December, they hold the capstone event for the year, the **St. Croix Marathon and Half Marathon**. Information for the race can be found at;
http://virginislandspace.org/stxmarathon2016.html

The marathon and half marathon are limited to 100 entrants each so anybody interested has to plan ahead. For those who are interested in any of the other races for the year, the complete calendar can be accessed from their homepage at
virginislandspace.org/

The calendar for 2017 is located at
virginislandspace.org/calendar2017.html

Chapter 8

Do Something Silly

For those who are young at heart, it is hard to accept that you are not supposed to enjoy the silly meaningless things you did when you were a kid. Free your inner self and just do them on St. Croix. For those traveling with young children, try to remember the silly things you did with your grandmother and share those family memories with your children.

Build a Sandcastle

Any time you go to the beach, you have an opportunity to build a sand Castle. It doesn't take much knowledge and there are video instructions on

Utube. The only three items you really need for the lowest level sandcastle are sand, water and molds. The water is necessary to make the sand stay packed in the shape otherwise when you empty the mold, you just get a pile of sand. Once you have the basics, let you imagination be your guide to building your own Castle in paradise.

Be careful when working around children as there are three kinds of behavior that are common; the helper, the ignorer and the destroyer. If you are working with a very young child and you get fascinated with your creation, don't be surprised when the child move quickly from helping you to ignoring you and finally destroying your fantastic castle in paradise.

But so what, building sandcastles is just plain silly as the wind, waves and the sun drying the sand will always destroy them whether you get angry or not.

On the other hand, building sandcastles is easy and very creative no matter what your skill levels is so have fun, take pictures and cherish the memories.

Live Life on the Edge

| Playing around on the edge! | Pensive on the edge! |

While hiking with friends and family on St. Croix, I have developed a knack for finding locations where the picture shows a dramatic scene of the subject being in a dangerous spot on the edge of a cliff. The pictures are staged to look dangerous but they are really an optical illusion. The visual effect occurs when there is an uphill walk to a flat plateau. If the photographer squats down, with the person standing at the edge of the plateau, it looks like life on the edge.

The pictures look so real that I got criticized after posting one on Facebook. The picture on the right is of my granddaughter living life on the edge and the critic thought I was irresponsible for not keeping her away from danger. Of course, there was no danger at all because the slope was so gentile, that she could have safely walked or even rolled down the very gentle hill.

Go to The Crab Races

Tito and Sue are hosts for the St. Croix's Crab Races three times per week. They show up with a 5 gallon bucket of Caribbean hermit crabs, Coenobita clypeatus, which are also known as soldier crabs. The crabs have a number on their back and come in all sizes. You pick your crab pay the entry fee and the crab goes in another bucket waiting for the race to start.

The race begins after everyone has made their pick and the crabs are dumped in the middle of a large circle. The crabs who win, place and show are the ones who exit the circle the fastest. The crabs are fairly harmless and well protected by their shell. Neither the crabs nor people are harmed in any way.

According to one promotional blurb; "It's great fun for all ages, there are lots of prizes to win, such as gift certificates for restaurants and activities, and there are toys for the kids to take home." The times I have gone to these silly events, most people are screaming and shouting for their crab to win and having a great time. Funny thing, unless you are jumping up and down you probably won't influence the crab very much either positively or negatively.

Hermit Crabs eyes developed for nocturnal vision so they don't have really clear vision and they don't have ears at all. They do see movement with their poor eyes but without ears, they sense sound by feeling vibrations. Let the kids on the other side jump up and down, vibrating the floor and scaring the crabs with their jumping and vibrations while you quietly wait for the crabs to come to you. Of course. this is not a silly way to act and have fun, so join the pandemonium and free your inner child

BTW, final hint, the smaller crabs, not smallest, seem to win more often, but they have many crabs in every size so knowing this does not improve your chances very much.

YOLO!!!

Pick a Coconut

There are two primary ways to use coconuts depending on the age of the nut. Old and brown coconuts can still be used for the meat of the nut, which is used in cooking, making candy and extracting the oil. Locally, the more common way is to harvest them when they are green and full.

A green coconut will have more fresher tasting coconut water and a small amount of jelly coating the interior of the shell. In St. Croix most coconuts are harvested for their refreshing coconut water, which is so pure that it has been used occasionally in the Solomon Islands to replace saline in blood

IV's. The National Institute of health has even published a paper on the topic.
https://www.ncbi.nlm.nih.gov/pubmed/10674546

In St. Croix, we drink it as a refreshing beverage or use it as a mixer for rum, gin or vodka. (It is allegedly a love potion.) Some of our local bars and restaurants will stock it but coconut water doesn't last long once out of the shell.

Probably the best place to get really fresh coconut water is from one of the many pickup trucks parked by the side of the road where a man will open the nut for you to drink the water, cut the nut in half for you to extract the jelly and even cut a piece of the shell to use as a spoon. The grounds keepers at local hotels and condominiums will generally offer a similar service.

Perhaps one of the sillier ways to do this is to climb a tree and harvest your own nut. Not only is this silly, it can also be dangerous. A fall of only 15 feet can kill or maim you and you will most likely be dead if you fall from a tree 30 feet from the ground. It's also valuable to know that people have been killed by falling nuts, so don't drop your prize possession. Moreover, you will probably be unable to get to the coconut water unless you have a machete and already know how to artfully use it to open the green nut without spilling the coconut water.

The picture that starts this section is of my very athletic and healthy niece climbing a tree. Young athletic people have a much higher survival rate after a fall from 30 feet. The picture above is of my daughter and I below my granddaughter, Ana, when she was less than ten. My son in law took the picture after yelling at me that if anything went wrong, he would use it as evidence when I was charged with child endangerment for allowing her to climb the tree. My daughter climbed trees starting at age 5 and my granddaughter also started at 5 years old so I was confident in her skills.

YOLO - you only live once!

Climb a Rock Wall

Rock Climbing can be a silly experience or just plain stupid. Many in my family and many others seem to gravitate to climb any apparently climbable surface. From about 5 years old, these intrepid beings want to climb trees, artificial walls, playground equipment and natural rock surfaces around roads and construction sites. In my family, there is rarely any intervention to stop the activity as all the adults did the same thing a generation earlier.

But watch out, not all of our exposed rock walls are stable. More than half the hills on St. Croix are composed of a compressed volcanic ash we call Rotten Rock. This rock is easily sculpted with a bulldozer to cut a flat surface to build a house on what previously was a steep hillside. Because the rock is brittle, the cut wall has many nooks and crannies that provide finger and toe holds, which facilitate climbing a very steep wall.

I anchored a repelling rope to provide safety for my granddaughters when climbing my hill. Of course my son, Andrew, had to show off and climb the vertical part of the hill. When my son-in-law heard, he had to do the same as pictured above. Naturally, my niece had to do it too. She got about ten feet up the hill and then trusted a loose rock, lost her balance and fell to the ground. While slightly stunned, all she had really suffered was a loss of dignity until another rock she had loosened came tumbling done the hill, hit her head and gave her a mild concussion.

You would think that that would dampen her enthusiasm for climbing but not in my family. A couple of days later we took a hike to the Salt River National Park. As we looked down on the waves splashing around a rock on the eastern point, I made the mistake of telling my daughter and niece that Andrew had also climbed that rock so naturally they accepted the challenge and had to do it. I got the previous picture and no one got hurt. The difference is that rocks along the shore are well weathered and most of the loose stones are gone. However, they can be slippery when wet causing another set of problems.

Walk on the Wild Side

The young lady in this picture had just graduated from college after working hard in high school. She was lucky enough to get a serious job offer and would return to a lifetime of work.

After visiting the beer drinking pig, we decided to stop at Cane Bay for a final drink at Sprat Net Beach Bar before returning to her room. While having her drink, she bemoaned the fact that she had never done anything spontaneous in high school or college and that she had been on St. Croix for a week and still had not done anything really spontaneous. Rhetorically, she asked why couldn't she just take off her clothes and run into the sea for a swim.

Calvin, the owner and the rest of the guys at the bar said there was no reason so go for it. She looked at me and I asked if her underwear was more modest than the skimpiest bikini she had observed on anybody and she said yes. So I said there would be no problem. She walked to the beach, got out of her clothes and walked calmly into the sea holding my hand while shouting for the world to hear;

"YOLO!, You only live once!"

What happens in St. Croix stays in St. Croix but we smile about it for months until the next funny story happens and then we move on.

Chapter 9

On the Serious Side

I never go on vacation to get depressed and I am pretty sure no one else does. With that in mind I have focused my energy on all adventures great and small found on St. Croix. I have focused on the beautiful, plants and scenery that can be seen on the island and our wonderful food and special events.

There are so many things to be enjoyed on St. Croix and the sea around it, I have purposely ignored all the stuff provided in tourist information on being under seven flags and the wonderful buildings of the Danish Colonial Era.

One exception for me is The Middle Passage Monument, which was unique to St. Croix, but has grown into a global movement of healing. I find the efforts made by a small group of people, addressing the issue of slavery without rancor, to be refreshing and uplifting. It is a positive movement, which should be attracting an even greater global following.

The Middle Passage Monument

It's a little difficult to describe how Toni Morrison, author and Noble Prize Winner, has a direct link to the St. Croix Middle Passage Monument. While the link is unknown to most students, residents and visitors, it has been noted in several scholarly works since 1999 that Toni Morrison was probably the first observer to go on record that there was no memorial for all the Africans lost at sea during the Middle Passage to Slavery.

It 1989, when Beloved by Toni Morrison was published, she dedicated her book to the 60 million who died as a result of slavery, which includes those who died in the Middle Passage and were "disposed of" at sea. Senator Wayne James of St. Croix took note of Toni Morrison's observation and a decade later started a project called the Middle Passage Monument to create a meaningful monument in remembrance of all who died in transit to the Western Hemisphere and while enslaved in the Americas.

James was first to develop the concept of a Middle Passage Monument as a tribute to the dead and inspiration for the living. Since this event, James has been credited in several academic books with initiating a global movement to pay tribute to those who died in the Middle Passage resulting in monuments in other locations (see references at end).

Monuments are now in Grenada, Savannah, Amsterdam and Africa. The United Nations is also in the process of building their own middle passage monument called Arc of Return by Rodney Leon.

Global recognition of Wayne James stops just short of a Nobel Prize. He was honored with the International Humanitarian Award, which has only been given out 12 times in it's 36 year history. Other past recipients include NASA, the Jacques Cousteau Oceanographic Institute of Monaco, and the Albert Einstein Institute for Advanced Studies at Princeton University. He was also awarded a Beacon of Freedom Award for his work in preserving African history.

The Middle Passage Monument on Queen Mary Highway in front of the St. Croix Educational Complex is an enigma to most people living on St. Croix yet may be the single most important sculpture of the twentieth century. Since it's mysterious overnight appearance in 2003, I have found it pleasing to the eye but never understood the significance until I took an art class at the University of the Virgin Islands with Cynthia Hatfield and discovered the complex meaning of the work for a research project.

I am familiar with the abstract sculptures and the classical sketches of Artist Mike Walsh, but the Middle Passage Monument is not easily classified. For me, it was simply one of those sculptures that I failed to understand because I was not aware of the intent of the artist. While I find it pleasing to my eye, I was trying to place the two large waves in the context of ocean waves of the Middle Passage, which doesn't really work. In my travels at sea, I have never seen opposing waves in deep water, well away from land.

Without understanding the intent of the artist, it is easy to critique it as art for the sake of art because it is attractive to the eye, however, that is not the true value of the work. When evaluated as a prop in a Performance Art Presentation by Wayne James, it may be the single most important sculpture of the twentieth century.

There are also two names for the sculpture. The original Middle Passage Monument was buried at sea as in memory of those Africans who died in the middle passage on their voyage to a life of slavery in the Western Hemisphere. The second monument, which was commissioned by Bermuda's Emperial Group and destined for that island, was renamed the Millennium Arch.

The Millennium Arch was supposed to be an exact duplicate of the original Middle Passage Monument, which had already been buried at sea. The copy destined for Bermuda has remained in its current location in front of the High School as a temporary storage site for over a decade and the ownership issue is still unresolved. This version was produced about 2000.

As positioned at the St. Croix Educational complex, the two arches seem to spring forth from the earth and the rather obvious focal point is the area enclosed by the two arches. In the center of that area, the viewer can see the entry-way to the St. Croix Educational Complex and viewed from the other side, the Campus of the University of the Virgin Islands.

In the view of the Bermuda Millennium Committee, the arch represents the flow of time. The superior arch represents the events of the past, which influence the future for all people depending on how they perceive history and teach it to their children. The smaller arch represents the events of the future. The gap between the two arches represents the present and our free will to decide how much of our past we will dwell on and allow to influence our future.

After discovering what I accepted as the intended meaning of the Millennium Arch, I absolutely love it. Partially, it is because of the hope it offers the world but equally important, for the hope it could offer our St. Croix students if used to its maximum potential.

In commissioning this work, Mr. James hoped to make the world aware of the horrors of the middle passage during the slave trade. James was hoping to promote peaceful reconciliation of the beliefs of the various races with regard to history.

In considering the contextual meaning suggested by Wayne James on the Middle Passage Website, the work would have to be considered a partial failure. I doubt that any of the current students on St. Croix understand the intended message and the hope it gives them for their own future.

While the work is aesthetically pleasing, it could be so much more inspirational and educational if it were used as part of a transition ceremony for those entering high school. (i.e cross under the arches, dispose of the worst of your past and work for the promise of your future). For that to happen, those in the administration would have to understand the work and its place in history.

However, when the Middle Passage Monument is considered as a prop in a Performance Art Show by Wayne James, it must be considered a resounding success. James got endorsements from the Congressional Black Caucus, the Nation of Islam, Christian Ministers and UN Secretary General, Kofi Annan.

He turned the dedication into a true media event. He dressed in white African robes and his entourage at the belated funeral procession was accompanied by wreaths, parasols, fan bearers, drummers and followed by a Tibetan Monk who struck a bell 400 times, once for each year of slavery. There was even an African spiritualist to communicate with the dead.

The artist for the arch was Mike Walsh of St. Croix who received a Bachelor of Fine Arts from Creighton University in 1971. Then in 1976, Walsh moved to St. Croix. In 1978, he began his own company, Walsh Metal Works and Gallery. He has exhibited extensively in St. Croix, including at the Fort Frederick Museum, the St. George Botanical Gardens and his own Gallery.

Walsh, works primarily in metal and creates site-specific installations placed amid the natural landscape of St. Croix. With each gust of wind, his distinctive pieces come alive as if they are living, breathing organisms intended to engage viewers in a cultural and ecological discourse.

After Bermuda publicly identified Mike Walsh as the artist of the Middle Passage Monument, Mike got some great publicity in an article in a Smithsonian Art Magazine by Renee Ater in "Slavery and Its Memory in Public Monuments." Special Issue on American Sculpture. American Art 24, no. 1 (Spring 2010): 20-23.

In preparation for an interview with Mike Walsh, I dropped off my original draft to him and we chatted about his experience in the Middle Passage Monument Project. Artist Mike Walsh attended the dedication and offered some personal insights.

The first mistake in my draft, which he pointed out was the "arch as a time line" was never his intention. As an artist he is pleased when others reinterpret his work in a way that moves them. Many abstract artists accept that it is ultimately the audience, which gives meaning to a work of art so Mike is pleased that the Bermuda Millennium Arch Committees found another positive meaning in his sculpture.

Mike's vision of his sculpture, as a monument to all who died during the Middle Passage and also, during slavery, has its roots in African and Afro-Caribbean religious beliefs and combines the beliefs of many different cultures. Religions developed in the islands based on the original beliefs of the people uprooted from Africa. They incorporated the Christian beliefs of the nationality of their new country so Haitian Voodoo is an African-Catholic religion.

Since the Africans were not all from the same tribes, Obeah of the English speaking islands would be African and Protestant in nature and incorporate different African beliefs because those captured came from different regions of Africa depending on whether they were enslaved by French, Dutch, English or Portuguese nationals. In addition, there is no set of orthodox beliefs in Obeah or Voodoo that all must adhere to so each separate group of believers have varying beliefs even in the same country.

Despite this complexity, there are some shared beliefs that helped guide Mr. Walsh:

- Death is not a significant ending but a transition from one part of the life cycle to another.

- Each man has a spirit, which returns to his community after death.

- Among many Afro Caribbean religions, adherents believe that after they die their spirit will return to their community in Mother Africa.

- Water, as a temporary home for the spirits, is a common theme.

An Arch is the strongest way to build an opening in a wall of stone or give a heavy roof support. The arch is used in religious buildings as a dramatic entrance way and for architectural support inside churches, mosques and synagogues. As early as the 14th century, the arch was placed on Egyptian Tarot Cards and when used in fortune telling, was associated with transitions in major life events.

Mike conceived his Middle Passage Arch as a portal to the watery world of spirits. The Arch would allow the living to interact with the spirits of their ancestors buried in the Middle Passage. In his mind, the Monument is a link between all African People and their ancestors.

The new UN project, the Ark of Return by Rodney Leon is thematically consistent with Mike Walsh's vision of a Monument for those who died in the Middle Passage. It is probably more than a coincidence that Leon is originally from Haiti where Afro-centric influences on Religion prevail. Leon's Abstract Ark is to carry the spirits of the dead back to Africa where they belong with their communities.

When Mike attended the Wayne James ceremony, he was moved by people who came the day before the event and stayed with the monument throughout the night. Some prayed before it and some prayed while leaning on it. All accepted the Arch for its intended use as a monument to those who died in the Middle Passage. While the ceremony sounded like Performing Arts to me, Mike said those in attendance thought it was a fitting and very moving spiritual remembrance for the dead.

Walsh built the second Arch on commission from the Emperial Group of Bermuda. No arrangements were made with him to handle crating and shipping the final Arch, so it stayed in his shop for a while. Eventually Walsh needed the work space and a no cost storage space was needed. Since Mike is a fan of Public Art, the solution for him was obvious.

Without asking permission, looking for publicity or waiting for a public dedication, he simply delivered it to the location in front of the Educational Complex and used temporary fasteners to secure it to the ground. He is a little surprised it has survived all our hurricanes since then.

There can be no doubt that patrons in Bermuda paid for the Middle Passage Monument in front of the St. Croix Ed. Complex. There is no dispute on the point of law. However, from an emotional perspective, there was a serious negative response from students when some representatives from Bermuda suggested they came to take it home with them. Since that one trip, no one has pushed the issue and it remains unresolved in a formal manner.

The following thoughts are excerpted from a 1999 report posted online by Andrew Williams Jr.

https://www.facebook.com/notes/andrew-williams-jr/1999-recap-bermuda-millennium-arch-committee-a-symbol-of-remembrance-and-hope-fr/10151656359744436

"The most compelling message of the Memorial is that we are living in a moment of exceptional historical transformation, where the consequences of past, present and potential future injustices are immediately sensationalized. The 16ft tall [brushed Aluminum] Arcs that constitute the Memorial represent the past and the future, while the "gap" between the Arcs represents the "present". The purpose of the Memorial is to crystallize externalized concepts of "space", "time" and "risk perception" in order to remind the observer that the choices we make in the "moment of decision" today will determine the destiny of our descendants...

We believe the Memorial Site must be dedicated as a Sacred Site and the Memorial treated as a Sacred Object. In classical cosmology the arch represents the crossroads between the realm of the living and that of the ancestors. It reflects the eternal movement of the soul as it proceeds from birth, life, death and re-birth. The Millennium Arch is a three dimensional cosmogram; a dynamic expression of this idea. The intersecting arcs serve as a gateway symbolizing the abstract forces of past, present and the future. Their collective energy and spirit thrusts upward out of the ground toward heaven to reclaim a place of primacy in the eye of the beholder. Simultaneously, we are encouraged to embrace the infinite possibilities of the imagination while also reuniting with the spirit of our ancestors whose lives have been absorbed by these forces."

Additional Reading:

Publications giving credit to Wayne James for starting the movement to create monuments, which honor those who died in the Middle Passage.

- "Monuments of the Black Atlantic" by Johanna C Kardux, "Blackening Europe: the African American Presence" edited by Heike Raphael-Hernandez (2004)

- "Disporic Slavery Memorials and Dutch Moral Geographies" by Joy Smith. "Essays in Migratory Aesthetics: Cultural Practices Between Migration and Art" edited by Sam Durrant, Catherine M. Lord (2007)

- "Toni Morrison's Beloved" by Justin Tally, (2008)

- Congressional Record, V. 146, Pt. 7, May 24, 2000 to June 12, 2000. "A bill to authorize the Homeward Bound Foundation to establish the Middle Passage Monument"

- Racial Justice Resource - Canadian Ecumenical Anti-Racism Network (2007) "Resources for Further Study and Learning", (Reference to Wayne James and Middle passage Monument) http://www.councilofchurches.ca/wp-content/uploads/2013/12/racism_racialjustice_part6.pdf

General References:

https://m.facebook.com/ComplexMassive/photos/a.104389529594437.7170.104387509594639/105268196173237/?type=1 This is the Ed complex photo, which is almost impossible to find, posted March 26, 2010, which states. The "first land monument is currently in the USVI at the Ed. Complex awaiting transport and dedication in Bermuda, the closest point to the actual monument."

Danish Colonial Buildings

It's an unusual contradiction in St. Croix that the government and historical societies work hard to preserve and perhaps even glorify the most oppressive era of Crucian History. I find the knowledge of the Amerindians who were trying to preserve their land and their way of life interesting. I also find the mysterious presences of the Knights of Malta fascinating and intriguing. However, all of the tourist landmarks that are on the must see list were built by slaves engaged in forced labor based on fear, intimidation and often brutal treatment.

Philip Freneau, "Poet of the American Revolution," left America for the West Indies in 1776 for two years before returning to get totally involved in the American Revolutionary War. He stayed for part of that time at Butlers Bay writing about the beauty of St. Croix. His poem, "The beauty of Santa Cruz" is 80 quatrains long and the first 69 are devoted to the fruits and bountiful harvests of the island and the wealth created for plantation owners. The last 12 are devoted to the plight and despair of the slaves of the island.
www.poetryatlas.com/poetry/poem/3737/on-the-beauties-of-santa-cruz.html

Freneau was familiar with slaves in America and may have even owned slaves as he was wealthy, but his experience in St. Croix changed his life. While on St. Croix, he sent a letter to a friend to describe "the cruel and detestable slavery" on St. Croix and wrote: "If you have tears, prepare to shed them now... no class of mankind in the known world undergo so complete a servitude..." After this observation of slavery in the Danish Colony, he became an abolitionist.

All of the following landmarks are impressive if you ignore the history of the era and the reasons for building them. Actually, this is fairly easy as your guide is not likely to explore the profits from involuntary slavery that built Whim, the background of the slaves that built Fort Christiansvaern or the fear that got Fort Frederik finished in 1760 after the 1759 slave rebellion.

In reality, almost every place on earth has a messy history when you dig deep enough. If we spent more time studying history, maybe we would spend less time repeating it, so enjoy the tours.

Fort Christiansvaern

The history of construction of Fort Christiansvaern starts with the St. John Slave Revolt of 1733. In brief, the slaves of St. John revolted, killed every soldier in the Danish Military Garrison and killed or drove away ever planter on the island including their families. They held the island in a self-sufficient manner for six months with dreams of retaining their own colony.

Danish officials appealed for help to French colonists at Martinique who responded by sending two French ships carrying several hundred well-armed French and Swiss troops to take control from the rebels. With their firepower and troops, they restored planters' rule to the island.

The loss of life and property from the insurrection caused many St. John landowners to move to St. Croix, which the Danish brought from the French the same year. While the planters found St. Croix to be a richer land, a fort to protect the island from pirates, slaves and other threats had to be built as the first course of action and slaves from the rebellious group recaptured on St. John were relocated to the isolated island of St. Croix and started construction in 1734. Fort Christiansvaern was finished in 1749.

Today, the fort houses the National Park's visitor center in Christiansted and according to their website, "The fort is a wonderful example of Danish colonial military architecture," which was primarily used as a prison for unruly slaves. The fort's cannons and guns have never been fired in an armed conflict. However, the prisons and dungeons were apparently well used.

Fort Frederik

From the start, Christiansted was perceived as the commercial center of St. Croix and the seat of government. It was a very easy port city to defend with at least 3 gun placements from the time of the French. The reef and the narrow channel were further barriers to invasion.

Frederiksted had no natural barriers protecting the deep water port and initially, there was not much to protect. As population spread out across the island construction was begun on Fort Frederiksted in 1752. It took fifteen years to complete the fort in Christiansted but after the slave rebellion of 1759, the work was rushed to completion the next year taking only eight years total using slave labor. The fort served the duel purposes, as a warning to pirates and a sanctuary for slave owners.

Nothing much happened at the Fort until 1776, when the Fort fired the first salute to an American Naval Vessel from foreign soil. The salute of the American brigantine at port in Frederiksted was a violation of the laws of Denmark's neutrality. Technically, it was a three gun salute suitable for a foreign merchant ship and not the 21 gun salute of a military vessel so there were no major ramifications. That was the closest the fort came to firing a gun during war.

The fort was stormed twice by rebellious slaves and capitulated both times. After a slave rebellion stormed the fort on July 3rd, 1848, Danish Governor Peter Von Scholten emancipated all slaves. The Frederiksted park adjacent to the fort honors the slave revolt leader General Buddhoe and also serves to recall and honor the 1848 proclamation by Governor Peter von Scholten.

After emancipation, nothing much changed and if anything, working conditions got worse. Thirty years later, in 1878, plantation workers dissatisfied with slave wages, set fire to much of Frederiksted without interference from the soldiers in the fort. The fort is a reminder of the only successful slave rebellion on what is now American soil. The fort is also home to the art and antique collections of Wayne James.

There are enough positive events, which happened here to make the $3 to $5 admission price a bargain. It is open weekdays from 8:30am to 4pm, and Saturdays from 1pm to 4pm.

Estate Whim Museum

In 1792, Whim was sold to Christopher McEvoy, a young man who had just inherited a massive fortune and a great number of estates in Europe and on St. Croix. He enjoyed his wealth in a flamboyant manner.

Born to the plantation life on the island of St. Croix, 33 year old Christopher was an experienced planter and slave owner who soon made

Whim a success. After his father had died in London, he became head of the family fortune. Christopher settled his father's Will and turned the operations of the shipping line and the European ventures over to his next oldest brother.

He returned to St. Croix and sold off his father's properties retaining only Whim. McEvoy built the Great House we see today and made many other major improvements at Whim. The slave houses were moved to the west of the Great House and made of stone. All of the roofs were shingled. He doubled the capacity of the sugar factory, doubled the number of slaves, and added a new still and a manager's house. He had a bathhouse built about 20 feet from the bedroom on the west end.

There can be no doubt that sugar plantations in the West Indies could generate massive wealth allowing the owner to live an opulent lifestyle and Whim preserves that lifestyle.

Chapter 10

Smell the Flowers

Plants in the Garden

The St. George Village Botanical Garden is located on the fertile central plain of St. Croix at the western end of the island. It is located in the area of an Amerindian Village, which was first settled over 2000 years ago. Near this spot, Ponce de León who explored Florida and Juan Garrido who was a free black African-Spanish conquistador made peace with the Amerindians in exchange for the Indians growing enough crops to feed the Puerto Rican conquistadors who were too busy, chasing Taíno women and hunting for gold in Puerto Rico, to feed themselves.

Shortly thereafter, Ponce de León left for Florida to find his Fountain of Youth and Garrido participated in the expedition led by Marqués del Valle Hernán Cortés to invade Mexico. The Spaniards who stayed behind in Puerto Rio invaded St. Croix and enslaved 147 peaceful Arawak Indians only to have the Caribs organize the Puerto Rican Indians and engage in battles against them for the next hundred years. Ponce de León got shot by a poison arrow and died in Florida. Garrido got married to an Indian woman in Mexico City, had three children and lived to be 70 years old with a pension from the King.

Plants in the St. George Village Botanical Garden are arranged along a thematic approach with herbs in one area, desert plants in another and orchids in their own house. The 16.5 acre garden site is planted among the restored buildings and ruins of the 18th and 19th century sugar cane plantation.

They have over 1,000 varieties of plants that demonstrate the horticultural potential for the U.S. Virgin Islands, while also emphasizing the ethnobiological value of plants as a source of food, medicine, fiber, color dyes, and building material.

St. George Village Botanical Garden has a collection of over 5,000 dried and pressed plant specimens, which represent about 80% of the plant species known to be growing in the U.S. Virgin Islands.

If you love history and flowers, this place is a definite must for your visit to St. Croix. You do a self-guided tour with a map and many of the more spectacular plants have placards of their common and biological names. Not all tell you why someone would have carried them to the isolated Island of St. Croix. You will learn a little more about that in the next section.

The Cactus Garden

The Orchard House

Books about St. Croix Flowers

I developed a late life interest in the flowers of St. Croix in the Botanical Garden and in the Wild. It seems that I needed to lose about 85 pounds and I needed exercise. I started walking and was bored to tears and then I started noticing all the beautiful flowers wherever I walked.

I brought my camera along and tried to identify the plants using Google Images on line. It was a hopeless endeavor. A search for Scarlet Trumpet Tropical Flower deliverers every color of the rainbow including some intricate passion fruit flowers, which are neither scarlet nor trumpet shaped.

I eventually learned that a good wild flower book is a fast track to identifying many flowers in a short period of time. The five books listed below are the ones I found most helpful:

200 conspicuous, unusual, or economically important Tropical Plants of the Caribbean
by John Merriam Kingsbury

My First Plant Book.

This book is a great first primer for anyone new to the world of tropical plants with a desire to identify them and where they come from. I live on St. Croix and most of these plants are present on the island. Kingsbury acknowledges the assistance that he received from the St. George Village Botanical Garden of St. Croix and staff members of the College [University] of the Virgin Islands.

Traditional Medicinal Plants of St. Croix, St. Thomas and St. John: A Selection of 68 plants
by Toni Thomas (Author)

A Great Introduction to Herbal Medicine.

I live in St. Croix so I purchased my book locally from the University of the Virgin Islands Book Store. I am glad to see that it is available to a wider audience through Amazon. This book is unusual for an Island Guide to Herbal Medicine. It not only tells the local use in the Virgin Islands but also other medicinal uses for the Greater Caribbean. Another desirable feature is that the book not only lists the positive benefits from use of the plants but also the potentially dangerous side effects. Far too often, herbalists extol the beneficial qualities of plants while ignoring side effects. This is a product of the University of the Virgin Islands Cooperative Extension Service.

Wild Plants of Barbados
by Sean Carrington

This Book Should Be Reprinted!

This is a fantastic book with pictures and descriptions of over 500 plants. I bought my copy years ago for about $20 but it is apparently out of print. Barbados uplifted about 600,000 years ago and is isolated in the Atlantic Sea. It is composed of a mixture of continental sediment and limestone similar to the central plain of St. Croix. Since there was never a land-bridge to the mainland or any other island, most of their plants were brought by Amerindians from South America starting 1500 years ago.

These facts make it similar to St. Croix so it is not surprising to find many of the same plants on both Islands and the other islands of the Lesser Antilles. The book provides medicinal uses for many of the plants and substantiates the claims with 66 scholarly references. No lover of tropical plants should be without this guide. Unfortunately, like many valuable books that are out of print, it might be cost prohibitive.

Tropical Trees of Florida and the Virgin Islands: A Guide to Identification, Characteristics and Uses
by T Kent Kirk

A Great Guide for Trees of the Virgin Islands.

To learn about the trees of the Virgin Islands, this is a great and inexpensive place to start. It covers 90 different trees with over 500 pictures. For each species, there is a description of the original origin, the plant, leaves, bark, flowers, fruit, habitat and uses. There is a list of twenty references used in writing the book.

The part that attracted me the most was the completeness of the section on the uses by mankind for the various trees and their parts. The author even has kind words to say about the usefulness of the very poisonous Manchioneel Tree.

The author also pays tribute to St. George Botanical Village on St. Croix and the staff at the University of the Virgin Islands. Margaret Hayes, Herbarium Curator, from the St. George Botanical Garden wrote the Preface to the book.

The Flora of St. Croix and the Virgin Islands Paperback
by Heinrich Franz Alexander Eggers

Eggers was the first to study and document the vegetation of the Virgin Islands. In 1876, he described the plants of St. Croix, and later in 1879 he expanded his work to include St. Thomas, St. John, Tortola, Vieques, and Culebra.

Baron von Eggers was a Danish soldier and botanist, who lived in the Virgin Islands from 1869 to 1887. In his Introduction to the 1879 book, he makes note of the isolation of St. Croix and did not cluster all the islands as one entity noting that isolated St. Croix was far different than Vieques, Culebra, St. Thomas, St. John and the British Virgin Islands.

He categorized the plants as being exclusively from St. Croix (115), common to the land bridge islands (221) [i.e. the rest of the Virgin Islands] or in all locations (667). His list includes 800 plants for St. Croix and about 900 for St. Thomas. Baron von Edgars was quite meticulous and my perspective is that he could not have missed 5000 additional species. Part of his low count is that the habitat for many plants may have been destroyed in favor of croplands for cane and garden crops and pastures for cattle. There would have been a natural recovery of some hidden plants as the island eventually reverted to a wild state.

After the American takeover of the islands in 1917, there were several waves or large scale immigration, which completely changed the demographics of the island. Just as with their ancestors, each wave of immigrants brought their plants with them. From Puerto Rico and Jamaica to the west of St. Croix and from all the islands of the Eastern Caribbean, people and plants came to the island increasing the biodiversity.

Many Americans and Europeans also came building houses and hotels and they brought the plants that they thought would improve the quality of life. This is still occurring to this day as some new plants have established themselves in the 35 years I have lived on island. This book is important as it establishes a benchmark inventory of species that were prominent before the American acquisition of the Virgin Islands.

Plants in the Wild

St. Croix is unique among the Caribbean Islands because of our Geography. All the islands on the Northern and Eastern edge of the Caribbean Plate were formed by volcanic action or partially formed by Volcanic action. Many still have active volcanoes. St. Croix is not on the plate edge and never had volcanic action.

Over the next thirty million years, coral beds started forming around the east and west end islands and silt from the erosion of the hills settled between the coral and the rock mountains. In the final uplifting about twenty-two million years ago, limestone marl was uplifted and filled in the middle of the two islands giving St. Croix the approximate size and shape it has today. Therefore, St. Croix shares the bedrock minerals of the Greater Antilles and the soil characteristic of the islands of the Lesser Antilles.

The Island of St. Croix was settled in several waves starting 5000 years ago. The first group of visitors were primitive Amerindians who left very little physical record of their presence. More advanced pottery making Amerindians arrived about 2000 years ago and created permanent settlements.

Around 800 AD, the Taíno culture started to evolve in Hispaniola and was labor intensive because of the need to support the ruling class. They immediately started a territorial expansion including Cuba, Puerto Rico and St. Croix where they assimilated the other more peaceful Arawaks who lived with a more egalitarian lifestyle.

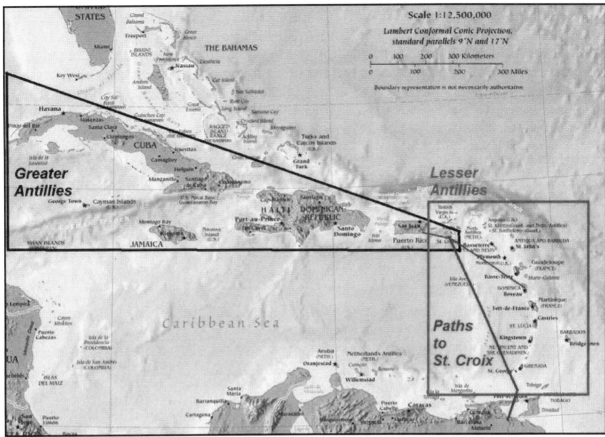

In school, most of us were taught that plants and animals spread to islands because of land bridges, floating seeds or were carried internally by birds. The problem with these theories is that St. Croix never had a land bridge to another island, there are approximately 30 floating seeds worldwide and our birds only eat about 30 different seeds and not all are native. World-wide the biodiversity of isolated uninhabited islands is always very low.

There are three plants, which evolved on St. Croix so that is not a major contribution to the biodiversity of our island, which includes over 6000 different species of plant life. These plants come from all over the world and were brought here by the men and women who came here to live.

By the time the Mayans established their empire and the Taíno and Kalinago inhabited the Caribbean, they had amassed knowledge on over 1500 medicinal plants, which was included in a written Mayan Pharmacopoeia. All copies of Mayan Medical Books were destroyed by the Spanish as they conquered and Christianized their New World.

The knowledge of medicinal plants today comes from efforts over the past 300 years to recreate the Mayan and Amerindian Pharmacopoeias. Part of it comes from gathering the knowledge of surviving herbalists among the Native groups and part comes from laboratory work on the medical effectiveness of the extracts of plants in screening tests. Once I have found the identity of a plant in St. Croix, it is fairly easy to find its global diversity and also the known medical information if any.

I really don't have a systematic approach to studying the plants of St. Croix. I start with plants that attract me because they are vines, those that caused an allergic reaction to me or those with beautiful flowers.

Most farmers hate wild vines so there would be little reason to carry them along on a journey and propagate them unless they had a medicinal or food value; Plants that cause a reaction are obviously biologically active and deserve a closer look; and flowers attract me because "the Almighty must have set his sign upon them" to do some good for mankind.

According to the early Christian vision of herbal medicine, the Creator had so set his mark upon Creation, that by careful observation, one could find all right doctrines represented and even learn the uses of a plant from some aspect of its form or place of growing. The theological justification for this philosophy was that: "It was reasoned that the Almighty must have set his sign upon the various means of curing disease..."

I am beginning to see in the plant history of St. Croix, that the Amerindians used a wide range of plants for every human condition. Ideas which are controversial to us today such as procreation, birth control, psychic visions, energy boosters and intoxicants are all part of their record and contributed to their survival and complex development. Following are just a few examples so that the plant record can speak for itself.

When humans started sailing the seven seas 50,000 years ago, a raft was probably the only flotation they had at their disposal, yet they made it from Africa to Australia probably by island hopping. Still, the unique mode of transportation led to a need for some standard and some unique medicines.

One of the more unique ones would be to cure seasickness. Not so obvious is that dysentery can be deadly if there is no ability to rehydrate with plenty of water. Finally, after sitting on a cramped raft, painkillers and substances to desensitize the body to pain would be valuable.

Dysentery is an intestinal inflammation that can lead to severe diarrhea. In some cases, untreated dysentery can be life-threatening, especially if the infected person cannot replace lost fluids fast enough and there is not much fresh water on sea voyages.

Ruellia tuberosa | Ixora coccinea

Ruellia tuberosa

In Asian traditional medicine, Ruellia tuberosa is used to prevent stomach problems and also as a painkiller and fever reducer like aspirin. The plant can also be used to reduce sensitivity to painful stimulus like sun and salt spray and as an anti-inflammatory for any skin problems. Animal studies confirm in technical terms that the plant has analgesic, gastroprotective, and anti-inflammatory properties. It also has been used to counteract the effect of poisons.

This plant is a native of North and South America but has been carried to Africa, Australia, and Indonesia.

Ixora coccinea

In folkloric medicinal uses, Ixora has been used for treating dysentery, diarrhea and associated colic pains. A decoration of leaves is used for wounds and skin ulcers. Powdered roots moistened with a little water on a piece of lint is also applied to sores and chronic ulcers. This plant is one of the oldest in Asian Folk medicine and has been carried to five continents as man spread across the globe.

Research studies provide a strong backup for the wisdom of the ancient people with regard to Ixora coccinea. Study of a root extract showed effective wound healing and antibacterial activity. The external application of the extract prevented microbes from invading the wound. An aqueous extract showed moderate inhibition against all bacterial strains tested. Like Ruellia, the extract was anti-inflammatory. It was also found to be a strong anti-ulcer compound like Tagamet. Results obtained in another study substantiate the anti-diarrheal effect of the aqueous extract and its use by traditional practitioners in the treatment of diarrhea. The list of therapeutic benefits seems to go on as it protects against chemical contamination of the body, acts as an anti-asthmatic agent and protects the heart. This is truly the wonder drug of ancient man and it is all over St. Croix.

Desmodium incanum

Desmodium incanum has been used as a diuretic and is good to settle the stomach including during seasickness. In Cuban folk medicine, it was considered an excellent hemostat, and was used in hospitals to heal wounds. It has been used as an analgesic and for fever reduction. Desmodium is thought to be a native of North and South America but also grows in Africa, Australia and Indonesia.

Rhynchosia minima

As tribes moved out of the African Homeland to populate the earth, birth control would have to become an issue. Australia was settled about 50,000 years ago and an ocean going voyage on a primitive raft would be a challenge even without a pregnant woman on board. Likewise crossing the Bearing Straight and fighting the mountains of the Continental Divide to populate the Americas would be far more complex and dangerous if the tribe was saddled with the burden of childbirth before they had found a place to establish a base camp.

Rhynchosia minima (Burn-Mouth Vine, jumby-bean, least snoutbean, rhynchosia) is used to control child birth. Established on five continents, it appears to have come out of the African Heartland and traveled everywhere that man has traveled except Europe. It has the same use everywhere. Modern journals of medicine describe it as an effective method of birth control for poorer populations who must rely on herbal medicine.

Stachytarpheta jamaicensis

Clitoria ternatea

Stachytarpheta jamaicensis

Stachytarpheta jamaicensis (verveine worrywine, snakeweed) is used as a sedative and to treat diarrhea, commonly drunk as tea – but lookout – the effect on blood pressure depends on dose and freshness with dramatic lowering or rising – implicated in throat cancer but might also have anti-tumor activities. Decoction or roots are abortive. On five continents including seafaring nations from Asia to Australia.

Clitoria ternatea

Clitoria ternatea (butterfly pea) - While supposedly an aphrodisiac, the roots are found useful to improve memory, intellectual power and as a sedative to increase sleep. As an aid to procreation, it is used in traditional Asian Indian Medicine to prevent habitual abortion. The roots of the white variety, mashed in milk are given orally to avert abortion and stabilize the fetus. This plant is on all of the inhabited continents except Europe.

Catharanthus roseus

Tradescantia spathacea

Anticancer

Humans have known about cancer for thousands of years, and excavation of ancient burials prove the presence of cancerous tumors on all continents in prehistoric times. Amerindians of North America had treatments for cancer hundreds of years before the arrival of Europeans who had no cure or effective treatments.

In 1955 the United States government established the Cancer Chemotherapy National Service Center, whose job it was to screen natural and synthetic substances for anticancer activity. Plants from around the world were tested, and hundreds of plants are now known to have some slowing effect on cancer growth.

Catharanthus roseus – Periwinkle

Catharanthus roseus, Periwinkle grows on all six inhabited continents. It has been cultivated for herbal medicine and as an ornamental plant all around the world. In Ayurveda (Indian traditional medicine) the extracts of its roots and shoots, though poisonous, are used against several diseases. In traditional Chinese medicine, extracts from it have been used against numerous diseases, including diabetes, malaria, and Hodgkin's lymphoma.

Herbalists are now constantly warned about the use of periwinkle tea for any reason because it is potentially poisonous. Meanwhile Lilly sells their periwinkle medicines whose side effects potentially includes death. However, the medicines usually appear to provide miraculous cures in many situations, so people take the risk.

The substances vinblastine and vincristine extracted from the plant are used in the treatment of leukemia and Hodgkin's lymphoma. This conflict between historical herbal use for treating the same disorders, and recent patents by Lilly on drugs derived from Periwinkle without compensation, has led to accusations of biopiracy.

In Voodoo, it is used as an incense and to promote love. It is banned by the state of Louisiana as a hallucinogenic although I found no other citations on this effect. Perhaps the Legislators of Louisiana believed love is a hallucinogenic experience, which should be banned for everyone.

Moses in the Rushes [Cradel](Tradescantia spathacea or Rhoeo spathacea) is on five continents as an ornamental or medicinal plant. In has been used in it's native Mexico as an anti-fungal and anti-Cancer drug and is still used in modern medicine as part of a treatment for cancer in that country. Naturally, it's use was documented in the Mayan pharmacopoeia, which people in Mexico, Belize, Guatemala and Honduras are working to reconstruct. The picture is in the safety section to demonstrate a skin rash I got from handling it.

Momordica charantia | Datura inoxia

Momordica charantia (Bitter Melon, Lizard Food, Jumbie Pumpkin or Cerasee) is one of the miracle foods of Herbal Medicine. It is eaten as a side dish because it is known to prevent and treat Malaria. Not so well known, the side dish is a strong treatment for diabetes.

It appears the vegetable attacks diabetes in several ways. Compounds in bitter melon have been found to activate the protein, which regulates glucose uptake; a process, which is impaired in diabetics. Bitter melon also contains a lectin that has insulin-like activity This lectin lowers blood glucose concentrations similar to insulin's effects in the brain, suppressing appetite.

Hallucinogenics

The use of any plant or substance to alter the normal state of mind is generally condemned by society unless it is being marketed by a pharmaceutical company for a profit. This consideration did not seem to be a major concern as early humans left Africa and populated the four corners of the earth. Leaders and spiritual guides routinely sought visions to seek out the best option for the group as a whole and many groups engaged in a transition ceremony for young men to determine what role they would play in the tribe as they mature.

There are many intoxicants, stimulants and hallucinogens in nature and St. Croix definitely has its fair share. While I have never found the plant, the National Park Service has identified Amerindian cocaine at Salt River and I suspect that people traveling 700 miles by canoe would rely on any plant that would work as a stimulant.

Although aware of the dangers, many native Americans have used plants as entheogens for hallucinations and rites of passage. An entheogen is supposed to generate the divine within a person. These plants are psychoactive substances used in a religious, shamanic, or spiritual context and can supplement many diverse practices for healing and revelation.

Datura inoxia, flower

As a genus, Dhatur species are hallucinogens with spiritual uses in pre-Columbian, North America, South America, Europe, Africa, Asia and Australia with no one quite sure where it originated. Its use has been documented for hundreds of years but because of the dangerous side effects, it is illegal to own, grow or use it in many countries. It was used in animal transformation rituals in North and South America, Africa, Central America and even Europe up until the 1600's when they tried 50,000 people in Europe and burned them at the stake for being Werewolves.

The name Datura, the genus name, is from the Hindu Dhatura, which was derived from the Sanskrit name D'hastura. This plant has been transported by man all over the world and as it moved to every continent, environmental adaption created nine species all of which are psychoactive and used by preindustrial mankind in a spiritual manner.

Datura metel is a closely related Old World plant for which similar effects were described by Avicenna in eleventh century Persia, and is one of the 50 fundamental herbs used in traditional Chinese medicine despite the danger.

Datura inoxia has been used by native peoples of the Southwestern United States in puberty ceremonies and in spiritual rituals. From historical accounts recorded by the Conquistadors, the Spanish conquerors of Mexico or Peru in the 16th century, we know that the Aztecs and other Indians, who had a detailed knowledge about numerous sacred and medicinal plants, were familiar with several types of Datura species.

This is a very dangerous plant where the active ingredient can vary five-fold from plant to plant and even vary that much on the parts of one plant. There are half a dozen plants on island that will kill you faster but Datura is the most dangerous for quickly destroying your mind.

Chapter 11

Your Personal Safety

Safely Walking and Hiking in St. Croix

When people think of wilderness hiking, they immediately think of snakes, insects, and like Dorothy in the Wizard of Oz, "Lions and tigers and Bears, oh my!" Put your mind at ease! St. Croix has no native snakes or dangerous wild animals and the worst biting insects are limited to a few spiders and the rarely seen centipedes. In 35 years of hiking, I have been stung only once by an insect other than sand flees and mosquitoes, which can be bothersome at night when I rarely hike. We do have bees and a local wasp and it was a wasp that stung me more than once. I had to take an antihistamine to suppress the swelling.

Still there are other hazards worth discussing, which include slipping hazards and the heat. Even the wild plants will wilt when it is hot and humid enough. The plants above normally have upward sweeping leaves. However, it was hot enough to see their leaves and small branches wilting towards the ground.

The key to safe hiking without falling is pay attention to the trail. With an easy walk in Estate Princess, there are no slipping hazards and only a few areas where branches have fallen and there is a risk of tripping on the flat terrain. For the Princess hike almost any shoes are appropriate and a walking stick is not essential although I always carry one. I prefer my Vibram Five Fingers shoes as they are like walking barefoot and along the beach I can walk on sand or in water and they dry quickly.

Moses in the Rushes

I always wear shorts and a loose fitting T-shirt so I don't overheat and pretty much stick to my Vibram Five Fingers shoes. My other pair of shoes are New Balance Sport Shoes, which are good for all of the hikes although I prefer "bare footing" on the beach areas. I always wear shorts and an old loose fitting T-shirt to help shed the heat and a hat to keep the sun off my head.

While exposure to the sap of many of our plants will cause a rash and if ingested, some plants can poison you, we have nothing as aggressive as the American Poison Ivy Plant and unless you wander off the trails, you are very unlikely to have a problem. One of my most serious skin rashes was localized to one arm and caused by excessive contact with a plant that is a common potted plant in America, Moses in the Rushes [Cradle]. Itching was eliminated by taking an over the counter antihistamine.

Our principle safety concern is the heat and "out of shape" people on vacation who are trying to overachieve. This is true for old men trying to relive their youth and healthy young people in the dead of winter who miss their normal aggressive outdoor activity.

The average high temperature in St. Croix is only 83 to 88 Fahrenheit with a maximum historic high of 97 (36 Celsius) in January of 1994. However, this balmy weather is deceptive. The temperature of the ground can easy reach temperatures in excess of 100 Fahrenheit and by radiation, the body feels these hotter temperatures. This measurement was taken on an overcast day when the actual temperature was closer to 85.

The other issue is the humidity, which is generally around 85%. The combination of Heat and Humidity makes dehydration a common event. On an easy Estate Princess hike, I usually don't prepare for dehydrating as the temperature under the forest canopy is five degrees lower than reported and about 25 degrees lower that the hottest road surfaces. The same is true of the moist beach sands. Still it is advisable to walk with a bottle of water.

Even when walking in town, it's is an excellent idea to remember to rehydrate and drink about one bottle of water every two hours and for longer walks pack a couple of candy bars to boost your energy.

I offer a final consideration even for a walk in town or on our beaches and trails. If you have known medical, issues check with your doctor before you plan your trip. Also, bring any medicine he advises to treat your potential problems such as an antihistamine or anything else your Doctor recommends. I am not trying to stop you from healthy exercise and a very good time, but no one likes to hear about our visitors hurting themselves.

Update on snakes:

For the same reasons that almost every plant had to be brought to St. Croix by humans, so did most animal life arrive at the hand of man. Iguanas were brought for food, deer were brought for hunting and meat and mongoose were brought to kill vermin. During the first 5000 years of human occupancy by Amerindians, Africans and Europeans, no one was dumb enough to bring snakes to the island.

Starting in 1990, there was a huge demand for construction labor to build large refinery units and also rebuild the island after Hurricane Hugo. Perhaps 10,000 people moved to the island to work. Most returned while others stayed and got jobs at the enlarged refinery or started their own construction businesses.

Dr. William Coles, chief of wildlife for the Division of Fish and Wildlife at the Department of Planning and Natural Resources on St. Croix reported that he caught the first imported red tail boa in 2008 but that increased to a few a year after 2012. All of them were sighted west of the Carlton area.

Coles believes they were originally brought in as exotic pets by someone who worked for HOVENSA. When the refinery closed in 2012, many workers returned to the mainland and some left their snakes and other pets behind.

The red tail boa feeds on native birds, chickens, rats, mongoose and small dogs. They are able to climb trees, making them a threat to native bird species.

The red tail boa is generally not harmful to humans. It can bite but it is not venomous. It hunts at night and hides out during the day. While not damaging to humans, the potential disruption to native birds, animals and pets is the reason for the attempted eradication of these non-native snakes.

Crime in Paradise

Any description of crime anywhere is bound to be influenced by the perspective and motivation of the person writing the report. In my case, I am a retired aging hippy, who has lived on St. Croix for over 35 years and never been a victim of a face to face crime. The same is true for my family. Yes, we have been rare victims of opportunistic crime where someone stole bikes from my yard or burglarized my business, but these are not confrontational type crimes that lead to violence.

When you think about any idyllic tropical paradise, it is hard to envision crime as an issue. Unfortunately, all of the factors, which contribute to crime in any large city are present in the islands. Most Caribbean Islands have severe economic inequality with the poor living in very substandard housing. Unfortunately, this housing is usually clustered in isolated villages or crowded projects.

The concentration of poverty facilitates drug use, personal gambling, teenage pregnancy, frustrated unfocused anger, criminal activity and a plethora of abnormal behavior mostly confined to these area of extreme poverty where both the criminal and victim are known to each other. It also extends to apparently irrational competition between poverty centers, called gang warfare, fighting for limited resources i.e. desirable women, superior reputation, a greater sphere of influence, etc. Pretty much the same is true in every large city with impoverished areas.

Crime in the Caribbean Basin is approximately the same on all the islands. I know that the last tourist murdered on St. Croix was about thirty years ago during a late night drinking party in the town of Christiansted during the holiday season. Still, I face the fact that St. Croix has a bad reputation and crime as an issue must be addressed. If you Google, "Tourist Murders on St. Croix", the Fountain Valley incident by disgruntled Vietnam Veterans dominates the search results, but that incident occurred 44 years ago.

As a comparison, I Googled tourist deaths in various Caribbean Islands over the past thirty years and while there are a couple that match our record of none, no one can beat us because zero is as low as it gets. BTW, I also Googled students murdered in various U. S. cities and also found that the number is rarely zero.

One reason tourist murder is low is that St. Croix generally loves tourists and no tourist has been killed in over 30 years despite our reputation. Much of what is appearing about crimes against tourists is simply not true and seems to be the deranged product of internet trolls and after the damage is done, Trip Adviser removes the false reports through a slow and tedious process.

I checked the advice to tourists for NYC and the same suggestions would apply here for the most part. To sum it up, avoid dark areas at night, leave your bling in the room, have wallets in front pants pocket, big purses should have shoulder straps, do not leave valuables in cars or on beach towels, don't talk to bums or hustlers, don't flash cash on the street. But remember trust your instinct. If it initially sounds like a con or too good to be true, it probably is. However, it is far too easy to skim over that paragraph so I will outline the NYC rules that apply to St. Croix, one by one.

Upon arrival, get your car at the airport and go straight to your room or hotel. Leave your luggage and valuables in your room and take the money or credit cards you expect to use with you. A large number of arrivals are late in the day when it is dark in winter so plan on eating a light meal in the vicinity of your hotel or room and start your exploring the next day.

If your room has a safe, keep your valuables in it. If your room has a peep hole, use it when you hear a knock at the door especially if you are not expecting anyone. If you can't identify the person at the door, call the front desk or the person in charge of your rental unit. Consider leaving your bling at home, St. Croix is a casual island and most people don't wear excessive bling.

Staying safe on the streets and sidewalks of St. Croix means being aware of your surroundings, developing good manners and using common sense.

1. There are many considerations about staying aware, which are distinctly St. Croix because of driving on the left. First off, always remember to keep left when driving even when turning at intersections. Perhaps the most difficult time to remember is at a traffic light with a right hand turn lane you must keep your body to the grassy side of the road on the left. Crudely stated by locals, this means "keep your ass to the grass."

2. It's also not intuitive that when walking on our roads you must walk on the right hand side so that you will see the traffic coming towards you. Before crossing a street, look both ways and if you see traffic coming from either direction wait until you see a break in traffic. Don't try to cross halfway because you might get trapped in the middle by cars coming from an unexpected direction. Fortunately, our drivers are usually polite and yield to pedestrians without any draconian laws or enforcement.

3. One friend who is 72 and pretty much deaf walks with a iPod on full

volume and rarely hears cars approaching from behind. Fortunately, he walks with me, so in an area where there are no sidewalks and occasional traffic, I scream at him to get off the road when a car is coming. The moral: pay attention to sounds while walking or walk with a "designated listener" who remains in touch with the surrounding sounds of cars approaching or aggressive dogs.

4. Walk with a walking stick. You will notice many people on St. Croix walk with a small stick or branch of a tree, which is used to back off the occasional stray dog. Some animal loving friends carry dog biscuits to feed the strays. I always carry a walking stick. Both methods work.

5. Walk like a local. Princess area is my favorite place to walk so when you walk or jog in these areas, watch what the locals wear and carry. No one has big cameras strung around their necks unless walking with a group; most people use iPhones or pocket cameras to take pictures. No one wears a lot of bling unless they are walking with a group. It is an old custom to say good morning, good afternoon or good day when you meet anybody while walking. Don't be surprised if people in their yards strike up a pleasant conversation. Don't be intimidated by someone walking on the wrong side facing traffic and coming straight at you. Just say good morning and if anybody asks for a dollar. Just tell them you never carry money when walking and keep going.

6. Develop your own key landmarks when walking or driving. Locals rarely use route numbers and GPS is not always correct mostly because of a lack of a uniform addressing system. Listen carefully when someone gives you directions. And be sure to write them down. The sad part, GPS locally is hit or miss for destinations so some people trust it until they try to find a person's house for an Old Year's Night party and get so lost that the host has to find a volunteer to leave the party and look for them. Old Year's Night is the local terminology New Year's Eve.

7. Once again, avoid dark areas at night, leave your bling at home or minimally in the room, have wallets in front pants pocket, big purses should have shoulder straps, do not leave valuables in a car or on beach towels, don't talk to bums or hustlers and don't flash cash on the street. But remember trust your instinct. If it initially sounds like a con or too good to be true, it probably is.

8. Unfortunately, young people are shooting each other in the projects and it occasionally rolls into the streets. So far no tourists have been accidentally shot on St. Croix and only one local innocent bystander, a friend, was killed in a botched robbery seven years ago by a ricocheted warning shot. With the gangs, the shootings are targeted assignation attempts, not random acts of violence. Of course, it is also not fun to be the victim of an armed robbery so just be careful where you go at night when walking to your car or take a taxi both ways. In the end these taxi drivers are good for something such as dropping you at a nighttime restaurant and getting you a ride back to your room. It will be expensive, you will feel cheated but you will arrive safely back where you started.

9. The more the merrier and the safer you are. Don't travel alone, find like-minded people and travel in a group.

There is no Paradise Island anywhere with a little man screaming "Airplane, Airplane" and where every problem is solved for every guest. There probably never was and probably never will be. But for those of us who live here and work here, St. Croix is pretty darn close to paradise.

View at Sunrise from Villa Boyd

Chapter 12

Villa Boyd on Judith's Hill
Christiansted, St. Croix, VI

When I first wrote this section about my Airbnb rental unit, I had no idea I was starting a book. I was just trying to be helpful to the people who were staying with me.

As time passed and guests asked me what to do on island, I started compiling a list and eventually decided to write a book for the larger audience of St. Croix Visitors. It turned out to be a much larger project then I thought because there is so much to see and do on the island.

I am happy to be a very small part of the Tourism Industry on St. Croix as most hotels, Airbnb accommodations and villa rentals receive excellent reviews. I would be proud if this book helped to make an exceptionally good Tourism Industry financially stronger and even better able to serve island visitors.

Since, I initially started compiling this book to serve visitors who stay with me, I am including the description of my efficiency in this Chapter. I am certainly not trying to imply that my guest accommodation is superior to our hotels. Depending on their needs and desires, my own family will stay in many of our finer hotels instead of staying with me and that is absolutely perfect for all of us when it happens that way.

Also, many of the units offered on Airbnb and for villa rentals are much larger than mine with multiple bedrooms but as shown in the previous picture very few will have a better view.

Congratulations if you chose Villa Boyd for your stay on St. Croix. My name is John Boyd also know as Poppa John (not the pizza maker) and I will be your host for the duration of your stay.

Upon Arrival at STX

The start of a great vacation starts with a pleasant arrival experience. Unfortunately, local laws and regulations prevent me from picking people up at the airport or providing taxi services while you stay with me.

However, I would be delighted to meet you upon your arrival in the baggage area of the airport. Since it takes a moderate amount of time for all of the bags to be offloaded from the plane to the baggage carousel, it is wise to start the car rental process first (unless you are renting from a company that doesn't have an airport location). While I give directions below, I advise you to have me come to the airport or car rental agency to greet you and have you follow me to Villa Boyd especially if you are not comfortable driving on the left hand side of the road.

Directions to Villa Boyd

All exits from the airport are towards the south. So as you exit the airport turn left (East) staying on the left hand side of the road and continue on "East Airport Road" (Rt. 64). This road parallels the runway you just landed on and will swing to the north at the end of the runway until it reaches a stoplight at "The Melvin Evans Highway" (RT. 66).

Continue across the highway on East Airport Road until the next light, which is the intersection with Centerline Road (Rt. 70); Turn right on to

Centerline while staying in the left lane. Continue on Centerline until you reach the second light, which is the intersection with Northside Road (Rt. 75). The exit to Northside Road is right before the second light. Watch out for merging traffic.

Continue on Northside road, which goes up and down and twists and turns for a little more than 4 miles. The road then intersects Rt. 751 to the left. There will be a restaurant, "Chocolate", just prior to the turn and "One Love" gas station after the turn.

Route 751 is the road to Judith's Fancy, a gated community. You will take the road to the third right hand turn where there is a sign for Pelican Heights and St. C condominiums on the corner. Turn Right and go about 200 yards and you will see a dirt road just after a tall telephone pole on the left hand side.

Take this road all the way to the end. There is a right hand turn in the road about half way up. The road dead ends at Villa Boyd.

Amenities of the Efficiency at Villa Boyd

If you are staying more than a couple of days, be sure to explore all of the drawers, and closets. The efficiency has been used exclusively for family gatherings prior to 2015 when I started on short term rentals. All my family members have different things that are important to their comfort. Over time there is quite a collection of "stuff" that you are more than welcome to enjoy.

As you enter, you notice the combined bedroom and sitting area. The books are mostly cookbooks with a few business books. Have fun and explore the library and even find a few good recipes. If you find something you want to try, I probably have spices that you can borrow for the duration of your stay to make something new and unique. For everyday cooking like tomato sauce, you can find bay, basil and oregano growing in my yard that you can pick and use.

Across, from the sitting area is a closet and the entry to the bathroom. Surrounding the sink in the bathroom are baskets full of goodies, just the type of stuff that TSA doesn't allow you to bring. There is bug spray, sun blocks of varying strength and various toiletries,such as soap, shampoo, shaving cream and toothpaste. I don't guarantee any consistent supply or brand as this is where I go when I run out. There are also first aid supplies in one basket and Aloe grows wild in my gardens. The raw aloe sap helps for sunburn but it will stain your clothes, Finally, there is a basket with a curling iron and other stuff.

The living room closet has a lot of stuff that is desirable for the beach depending on how much you want to carry with you. There are two different sized coolers and a few jugs for liquids such as sangria. Yes, you can carry alcoholic beverages to our beaches, but not into somebody's bar or restaurant area. There is an old beach bag and some big hats to provide shade at the beach. At the bottom left there are some old towels, which can be used for the beach. Leave the good dark blue bath towels in the room. For those planning a big beach party the red quilt on the bottom shelf and the cushion above it are there to be used outside. For a picnic, this is almost essential as almost anywhere you sit on the ground with food, ants will find you. For those who prefer beach chairs, there are two in the front closet by the door.

Some rental accommodations will be sure to offer more and others less. Be sure to read the customer reviews on Airbnb and Trip Adviser before picking your accommodations and if something is important to you be sure to ask you host to see if your special needs can be met. On St. Croix, more often then not, the answer will be yes no matter where you stay.

Have a great vacation and remember, I hope you have a wonderful time on your St. Croix Vacation and enjoy many of our varied activities. After your fantastic Vacation, I hope that you have learned to love St. Croix as much as I do.

I can be contacted at villa.boyd@gmail.com

Made in the USA
Las Vegas, NV
28 January 2021